H. LEVITSKY

KIEV

a short guide

MISTETSTVO PUBLISHERS
KIEV

PROGRESS PUBLISHERS
MOSCOW

1980

Генрих Юзефович Левицкий

КИЕВ
Краткий путеводитель

На английском языке

Редакция литературы по спорту и туризму

Translated from the Russian by *Angelia Graf* and *Christopher English*
Editors of the Russian text *Es. Umantseva*, *V. Ostroumov*
Editor of the English text *G. Pavlov*
Designed by *N. Nesterenko*
Art Editor *Y. Malikov*
Lay out by *G. Kalintseva*
Maps by *L. Cheltsova*

Updated to March 1, 1979

Л $\frac{20904-031}{014(01)-80}$ 91—80   1905040100

Contents

Kreshchatik Street, Kiev's main thoroughfare

COME TO KIEV

As you take your first steps in our city from an airplane ramp or an express train, Kiev welcomes you and presages many interesting meetings and discoveries during your stay.

Kiev is the capital of the Ukrainian Soviet Socialist Republic, one of the fifteen equal Soviet constituent republics and a founding member of the United Nations Organisation. The nature and tempo of life in the city fully accords with its status as a political, administrative, economic, scientific and cultural centre. Located in Kiev are the Central Committee of the Communist Party of the Ukraine, the Supreme Soviet of the Ukrainian SSR, the Council of Ministers of the Ukrainian SSR, the Ukrainian Republican Trade Union Council, the Central Committee of the Leninist Young Communist League of the Ukraine, various ministries, departments and societies, and a whole number of foreign consulates. A considerable portion of the republic's industrial might is concentrated in Kiev, which has well-developed machine-building, precision electrical instruments and light industries. The capital is also the seat of the Academy of Sciences of the Ukrainian SSR; dozens of research and design organisations, the republican boards of artistic unions, 18 institutions of higher learning, seven theatres, a radio and television centre, publishing houses and film studios, several major

libraries and museums housing precious collections, and
extensive sports facilities.
Kiev's history spans fifteen centuries, full of dramatic
events and heroic deeds. For centuries it was the gold-domed
capital city of Kievan Rus, the cradle of the fraternal
Russian, Ukrainian and Byelorussian peoples. Here outstanding
philosophers, artists, architects, poets, scholars
and revolutionaries dreamed of a radiant life to come.
On more than one occasion the city was razed to the ground
by foreign invaders, but again and again it rose from
its ashes. Its architectural monuments, the pride of
the nation, are now famous throughout the world.
Kiev has a vivid revolutionary past. In bronze and granite the
city has perpetuated the memory of the Decembrists, Russian
revolutionaries from the nobility who   started the first
armed uprising in Russia against tsarist autocracy in
December 1825; of the heroes of the 1905 Revolution; of
the Kiev workers, ardent fighters in the October (1917)
and January (1918) armed uprisings, who bravely followed the
Russian proletariat in raising the banner of the Great
October Socialist Revolution.
Kiev is one of the Soviet hero cities. Its
courage and valour played an outstanding role in the
Soviet people's Great Patriotic War against the nazi
invaders.
Kiev is a city of lively housing estates on the picturesque hills

and plains bordering the Dnieper. It now extends more than fifty kilometres along both banks of the river. Woods, parks and public gardens make up over half its area of nearly 80,000 hectares.

The flag of Kiev bears two Orders of Lenin and a Gold Star medal, testimony of the city's working people's great services to the socialist state.

The monument in Honour of the Great October Socialist Revolution

The building of the Supreme Soviet of the Ukrainian SSR

The building of the Executive Committee of the city Soviet of People's Deputies

Kreshchatik celebrates

The Rusanovka Canal ▶

The Ukrainian Trade Union Council building   *The Dnieper's left bank*

The monument to Taras Shevchenko

The Hotel Kiev ▶

THE GATEWAYS
TO KIEV

BORISPOL AIRPORT

(35 km southeast of Kiev along
Kharkov Highway; scheduled
buses, route taxis)

This major international airport is named after the ancient town of Borispol, which lies nearby. Airlines from socialist countries, like LOT, MALEV, Interflug, Balkan, CSA and JAT, have flights to Borispol and planes from Moscow headed for Montreal, Paris and Zürich and vice versa make transit stops here. Liners manned by Borispol crews fly to seventeen countries, to cities such as Budapest, Warsaw, Berlin, Prague, Sofia, Vienna and London. Kiev also has uninterrupted aerial communication with the Soviet Union's largest industrial and cultural centres. Passengers are served by the comfortable TU-124, TU-134, TU-154, YAK-40, IL-62 and other liners.

The airport is equipped with the most up-to-date engineering, radio-technical and meteorological systems and can thus receive all existing kinds of planes.

The modern-style terminal building, which is both functional and attractive, is the pride of Kiev architects. Its spacious rooms

contain service sectors, an extensive network of communications and information services, lounges, make-and-mend service shops, restaurants, cafeterias, bars and various kinds of kiosks. The right wing of the building houses an international sector, where Intourist premises, rooms for members of the diplomatic corps and the offices of airlines from the socialist countries are located.

Besides Borispol Airport, Kiev is served by the Zhulyany air terminal, which is mainly used for intra-republican flights. The two airports receive and see off over five million passengers a year.

The staff of the international sector of the Central Agency for Aerial Communications will help foreign passengers with their travel documents and tickets for all of Aeroflot's international and national flights and for all planes leaving Soviet airports.

Borispol Airport, International Sector—tel. 267243

Zhulyany Airport, International Sector—tel. 712460

Central Agency for Aerial Communications, International Sector—tel. 744223

THE CENTRAL
BUS TERMINAL

The Bus Terminal platforms

(3 Moskovskaya Ploshchad;
trolleybuses 1, 11, 12 to the city
centre)

The Central Bus Terminal, an
important junction of bus routes
from all regions of the Soviet
Ukraine and a large number of cities in the Russian Federation, the
Byelorussian SSR and the Molda-
vian SSR, has more than 400 in-
coming and outgoing buses a day.

There are altogether five inter-
city bus terminals in Kiev.

The city's bus stations have 68
inter-city routes with an overall
length of more than 24,000 kilometres, as well as 100 suburban
and inner-city routes. The inter-
city routes are served by the Kiev,
Lybid, Darnichanka and Zhovt-
nevy bus lines. You can also tour
the Ukraine's historic and other
sights aboard the comfortable
express buses.

Express tourist buses also link
Kiev and the Hungarian People's
Republic, the German Democratic
Republic, the People's Republic
of Bulgaria, the Polish People's

The Railway Station

Republic and the Czechoslovak Socialist Republic.

Rationally distributed among the Central Bus Terminal's three storeys are booking offices, a waiting room, restaurant and hotel. The interiors are decorated with views of Kiev done in mosaics in a folk art style.

Controller's office—tel.634127, 637180

Central taxi bureau—tel. 082

THE RAILWAY STATION
(Vokzalnaya Ploshchad; Vokzalnaya Metro station)

Kiev is a major national and international transport junction. In spring and summer, at the height of the tourist season, about half a million travellers arrive at the Kiev railway station every day. It serves as a point of departure, transit stop and final destination for special, international and long-distance trains. The capital of the Ukraine has railway connections with the most distant areas of the Soviet Union and many countries of Europe and Asia. From here you can travel direct to Warsaw, Berlin, Sofia, Prague, Budapest, Bucharest, Belgrade, Vienna, Paris, Stockholm, Rome, Athens, Istanbul and Ulan Bator. The Kiev branch of Intourist arranges the travel documents for international trains and carriages.

The station building itself, which was erected in 1932 and occupies a prominent place in the

city's architecture, has been reconstructed several times to keep up with the rapid growth of railway transport. The huge lobby is conveniently connected by passages and stairways with the waiting-rooms on the first and second floors, with the cloakrooms and platforms, the restaurant and the gallery built over the tracks, and holding about a thousand persons. Near the central entrance to the station you will find an excursion office of the Kiev Travel and Excursion Bureau. A short distance away is the suburban train station, from where you can leave on an interesting trip to the picturesque environs of Kiev.

Information—tel. 005

The berths of the river station

The Vokzalnaya Metro station

THE RIVER STATION

(Pochtovaya Ploshchad; Pochtovaya
Ploshchad Metro station)

The Kiev River Port is one of
the largest on the Dnieper. Each
year this modern concern hand-
les large numbers of passengers
and millions of tons of various
freight.

A genuine revolution occurred
in transport on the river with the
appearance of high-speed hydro-
foil boats. The Kiev River Station,
commissioned in 1961, serves
long-distance passengers on such
vessels. The first two storeys are
given over to administrative and
auxiliary premises, booking-
offices and cloakrooms. On the
third and fourth floors are waiting-rooms, a hotel and a restaurant. Particularly noteworthy in
the interior decoration are the or-
namental panels "From the Va-
rangians to the Greeks", "Bogdan
Khmelnitsky's Arrival in Kiev",
"The Establishment of Soviet
Power in the Ukraine", "Industry
on the Dnieper", "Relaxing on
the Dnieper". The suburban pavilions, from which one can depart

The excursion ship Yevgeny Vuchetich

on an interesting tour of the Dnieper's nearby coves, share the main station's platform.

The comfortable four-deck motor ships *Yevgeny Vuchetich* and *Sovietskaya Rossiya*, each accommodating 360 passengers, make cruises along the Dnieper through the central and southern Ukraine. The ships have one, two and three berth cabins with air conditioners and all that is needed for a comfortable journey.

River Passenger Transport Agency—tel. 361268, 367111.

THE LANDMARKS
OF THE ANCIENT CITY

THE GOLDEN GATES

(corner of Vladimirskaya and
Yaroslavov Val Streets;
trolleybuses 4 and 12 from
the Bus Terminal, trolleybus 2
from the Railway Station, bus 71
from the River Station)

Kiev's Golden Gates date from the 11th century. Surrounded by a picturesque public garden, they, like other monuments of the past, are carefully protected by the state. It is from here that tourists usually begin their rounds of Kiev of the times of Prince Yaroslav the Wise, under whom Kievan Rus reached the height of its flowering and might.

The Golden Gates were a monumental structure, 7.5 metres wide, with a 12-metre-high and approximately 25-metre-long passage, which served both as the main entrance to the central part of the capital's citadel and a mighty defensive barrier. Their dual purpose, by analogy with the Golden Gates of Constantinople, and perhaps also the fact that the grand entranceway's oaken doors were reinforced with copper and decorated with precious metals were what gave the gates their name. Judging from chronicles, the Golden Gates were a rectangular, two-tiered structure with Church of the Annunciation over the entrance. Their walls were built of natural stone—granite, quartzite and slate—and plinths of large, flat bricks laid in pink mortar. The alternation of brown-red and grey-green stone with strips of pink mortar, and the decorative, semi-circular niches in the wall gave the building a particularly attractive appearance. The Golden Gates were damaged during the Mongol-Tatar invasion of 1240, but continued to serve as the entrance to the city until the mid-seventeenth century. In order to preserve them, the remnants of the ancient monument were covered with earth in 1750. In the 1830's they were excavated by the Kiev archeologist K. Lokhvitsky, and somewhat later measures were taken in consultation with the architect A. Beretti to conserve the ruins. Today all that is left of the Golden Gates are fragments of the two parallel walls, which give an idea of stone-laying techniques in Ancient Rus. Projects have now been drawn up to restore this architectural monument.

The Golden Gates. 11th century

THE ST. SOPHIA MUSEUM

**(24 Vladimirskaya Ulitsa;
trolleybuses 2, 4, 12;
buses 20, 38, 68, 71)**

In 1934 this unique complex of 11-18th-century buildings acquired the status of a State Museum of Architecture and History by decision of the government of the Soviet Ukraine. A magnificent example of ancient Russian and Ukrainian architecture, it covers an area of five hectares in the centre of Kiev.

The crowning glory of the en-

A bird's-eye view of the St. Sophia museum

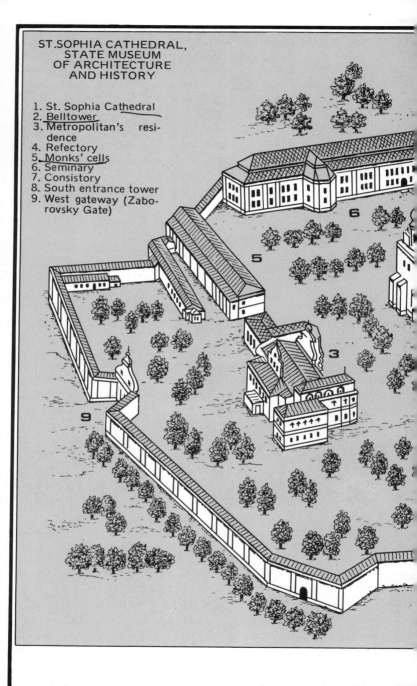

ST. SOPHIA CATHEDRAL,
STATE MUSEUM
OF ARCHITECTURE
AND HISTORY

1. St. Sophia Cathedral
2. Belltower
3. Metropolitan's residence
4. Refectory
5. Monks' cells
6. Seminary
7. Consistory
8. South entrance tower
9. West gateway (Zaborovsky Gate)

The St. Sophia Cathedral, an 11th-18th centuries architectural monument

semble is the St. Sophia Cathedral. The foundations of this multi-domed, five-naved church with its open gallery were laid by Prince Yaroslav the Wise in honour of his victory over the Pechenegs, and it was then erected by unknown masters in 1037. The Cathedral stood out among the other buildings of "Yaroslav's Town" for its particular grandeur. As Russia's main metropolitan church, it was to symbolise the wisdom of Christian dogma and affirm feudal princely power. At the same time the Cathedral was the centre of the ancient Russian state's social and cultural life. It witnessed the ceremony of the princes' "seating" on the throne, the debating of the Kiev *veche* (popular assembly), receptions of West Euro-

pean sovereigns, dynastic rituals, the beginnings of chronicle writing, the founding of the first Russian library, and popular festivities. In the course of its existence, St. Sophia underwent many enemy attacks, partial destruction and reconstruction, but retained its original appearance up to the 17th century, as some sketches by the Dutch artist Abraham van Westervelt dating from 1651 testify. Major repairs undertaken in the late 17th and in 18th centuries radically changed the Cathedral's external appearance. Six cupolas were added to the original thirteen, and the contours of the main domes were changed to give them the pear-shaped form characteristic of Ukrainian architecture of the period. It was also at this time that second storeys were built over the Cathedral's external galleries. In 1889 St. Sophia's west façade was entirely rebuilt, a narthex was added, and the 18th-century baroque pediment was replaced by an arched one. This is the form in which the Cathedral has come down to us.

As you cross the Cathedral's threshold, you are immediately overcome by its grandeur and splendour. Its majestic size (length—37 metres; width—55; height from the floor to the top of the central cupola—29), severe inner proportions and monumental wall decorations (260 square metres of mosaics and about 3,000 square metres of frescoes) dating from the 11th century overwhelm you with their perfection "before you can even see and grasp all the details and understand all that the creators of this masterpiece of architecture and painting wanted to say", as the prominent Soviet historian B. Gre-

kov once said. The mosaics of Christ the Pantocrator, the Mother of God (Orante), the Annunciation, Deisus and Eucharist never fail to captivate visitors. Equally famous are the frescoes depicting ancient sporting contests, hunting scenes, performing jesters and so on. There is also a mural of the numerous family of Prince Yaroslav the Wise. You may be interested to know that the Grand Prince's daughters became queens of Norway, France and Hungary, that Yaroslav himself was married to a daughter of the Swedish king Olaf, that his sister married the Polish king Cazimir I, that his sons Svyatoslav and Vsevolod married Byzantine princesses and that the famous Norwe-

The main entrance to the St. Sophia Museum

"Christ the Pantocrator". 11th-century mosaic

gian Vikings Olaf the Saint, Magnus the Good and Harold the Hard Ruler as well as the English king's sons and the heir to the Hungarian throne Andrei I found political asylum at Yaroslav's court. The court thus had truly extensive dynastic ties, and this contributed to enhancing the international prestige of the ancient Russian state.

For a long time the St. Sophia Cathedral served as the burial place of the Kiev princes. It was here that Yaroslav the Wise, Vsevolod Yaroslavich, Rostislav Vsevolodovich, Vladimir Monomakh and other Kiev rulers were buried. But only the marble sarcophagus of Yaroslav the Wise, an object of great historic and artistic value, has been preserved to this day.

On your tour of the Cathedral, do not fail to have a look at its south side-chapels, which made their appearance after the 17th- and 18th-century reconstructions and now house a collection of 12th-century mosaics and frescoes, which were carefully removed by Soviet restorers from the walls of St. Michael's Cathedral (sometimes called the Golden Heads) which could not be saved from destruction.

On the territory of the museum there are quite a number of 18th-century buildings, which form an ensemble characteristic of Ukrainian monasterial architecture of the period. The 76-metre-high, four-tiered belfry, with a gilt, pear-shaped cupola, which now towers over the whole group of structures making up the museum complex, was frequently reconstructed and repaired after it was built between 1699 and 1706. In 1709 at the foot of the belfry the inhabitants of Kiev triumphantly greeted the victors of the Battle of Poltava, headed by Peter the Great, who had routed the troops of the Swedish king Charles XII, and so it is also called the Triumphal Tower. To its south lies the monastery refectory, to the southwest, the consistory, to the north, the seminary

"Bear hunting". 11th-century fresco

and monks' cells, while opposite the main entrance to the St. Sophia Cathedral is the Metropolitan's residence. The entire compound is surrounded by a stone wall, which had three entrances in the 18th century: under the belfry, under the south entrance tower and through the west gateway, or so-called Zaborowsky Gates, named after the Kiev Metropolitan Rafail Zaborowsky, under whom many churches were built in the city.

The St. Sophia Cathedral is a State Museum of Architecture and History, affiliated to which are the churches of St. Cyril and St. Andrew in Kiev, the Sudak fortress in the Crimea and the Chernigov preserve. All these monuments attract an incessant flow of tourists, but the St. Sophia Cathedral remains the most important, most prized and most popular among them, with about two million Soviet and foreign visitors a year.

St. Sophia Cathedral Museum— tel. 296152

THE KIEV-PECHERY LAVRA

(21 Ulitsa Yanvarskovo Vosstaniya; trolleybus 20)

In 1926 this unique group of 11-18th century buildings acquired the status of a State Historical and Cultural Museum by decision of the government of the Soviet Ukraine. The complex covers an area of 28 hectares; forty of its one hundred stone structures are valuable specimens of 11-12th and 17-18th-century architecture and art. The Church of Our Saviour in Berestovo, the Trinity Gateway Church, All Saints Church, the Church of the Exaltation of the Cross and the Near and Far Caves are open to the public.

The museum embraces the territory of the former monastery, first mention of which is found in the famous chronicle *Povesti Vremennykh Let* (The Tale of Bygone Years) among the entries for the year 1051. The origins of the monastery, which is called by the Byzantine name of Lavra, are linked with the spread of Christianity in Russia. In ancient times it was a leading cultural centre, where the chroniclers Nestor, Nikon and Iakov lived and worked, as well as the painter Alipi and the physicians Agapit and Damiant, who made a notable mark in the history of Ancient Rus. The monastery buildings, like the whole of Kiev, were subjected to destruction on more than one occasion, but with the passage of time they again rose from their ruins and ashes, resurrected by talented artisans. The monastery acquired its final architectural form in the second half of the 17th and early 18th centuries, a time of economic, political and cultural growth stimulated by the Ukraine's reunification with Russia.

The Kiev-Pechery Lavra's main shrine was the Cathedral of the Dormition, which was built and decorated in 1073-1089. This six-pillared, single-cupola, stone church was notable for its luxuriance and wealth of decorations, and as an annalist testifies, it was "like onto the heavens". Particularly impressive were the gorgeous, multi-tiered iconostasis, the carved and gilt interior and the inlaid marble floor. After being ruined during the Mongol-Tatar invasions, the cathedral was restored in 1470. Its interior and exterior decorations were subsequently destroyed in a 1718 fire; the cathedral was then rebuilt between 1722 and 1729 under the supervision of the Russian master I. Kalandin into a large, two-tiered church with seven cupolas and rich interior and exterior decorations. In the 1760's the monastery's talented serf architect Stepan Kovnir added figured pediments over the cathedral's top cornice, while the sculptor Iosif Belinsky contributed stucco ornamentations. The Cathedral of the Dormition with its wealth of artistic treasures was destroyed during the Great Patriotic War. Only an insignificant part of it remains, but this is enough to give one a general idea of what this outstanding architectural monument was like.

The main entrance to the monastery is surmounted by the harmoniously proportioned and richly ornamented Trinity Gateway Church, which was built in 1108. Following the 1718 fire, the church was somewhat reconstructed in the 1730's, and in 1731 it was finely decorated by the talented master Vasily Stefanovich. Wave-like pediments were added to the small, four-pillared church and the drum of its single cupola was effectively decorated with stucco ornaments and coloured ceramic rosettes, characteristic of the Ukrainian baroque style. The murals on the façades and interior walls of the church were executed in the first half of the 18th century by masters of the monastery's icon-painting school. The emerald green of the walls combined with the gilt lace of the cornices strikes a forceful major chord against the background of the severe fortification walls.

The Trinity Gateway Church, a priceless specimen of ancient Russian architecture, has remained well-preserved to this day.

The museum also includes the Church of Our Saviour in Berestovo, built in the late 11th and early 12th centuries in the village of Berestovo, which served as the Kiev princes' out-of-town residence. It was a large, six-pillared church with three apses, which was girt by a meander brick frieze and crowned by a drum with a semi-spherical cupola. The church is decorated with a profusion of frescoes. The genre scene, "Christ Appears to His Disciples on Lake Tiberias" is notable for its dynamic composition and free style of painting, and the frescoes of the Annunciation and the Nativity are quite expressive. The 17th-century fresco portrait of the Kiev Metropolitan Pyotr Mogila by a Ukrainian artist is outstanding for its depth of characterisation. It is under Pyotr Mogila that the church, also destroyed during the Mongol-Tatar invasions, was rebuilt in 1644. The Greek masters he invited for the purpose were

The Lavra's Great Belfry dates from the 18th century

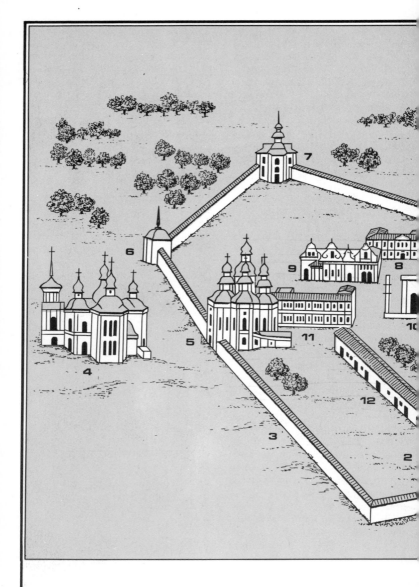

KIEV-PECHERY LAVRA

1. Trinity Gateway Church 2. St. Nicholas Church 3. Fortress Walls 4. Church of Our Saviour in Berestovo 5. All Saints Church 6. Malyarnaya Tower 7. Onufri Tower 8. Lavra Printing house 9. Kovnir Building 10. Church of the Dormition (ruins) 11. Economic Building 12. Monks' cells 13. Great

Belfry 14. Monks' cells 15. Kushnik Tower 16. Governor-General's residence 17. Clock Tower 18. Metropolitan's residence 19. Refectory (nearby are the graves of I. Iskra and V. Kochubei) 20. Belltower in the Near Caves 21. Church of the Exaltation of the Cross 22. Church of the Conception of St. Anne 23. Belltower in the Far Caves 24. Church of the Nativity of the Mother of God.

The All Saints Church and the Economic Building. 17th-19th centuries

The Church of the Nativity of the Mother of God. 17th century

The Church of Our Saviour in Berestovo. 11th-19th centuries

able to splendidly harmonise their new paintings with the church's internal architecture. In ancient times the church served as the family sepulchre of the Monomakhovichi princes, and the son of Vladimir Monomakh, the Kiev Prince Yuri Dolgoruky, who is known in history as the founder of Moscow, was buried here in 1157.

The monastery's Great Belfry soars high above all its other buildings. With its height of 96.52 metres, it used to be the tallest tower structure in Russia. Completed in 1744 under the direction of the famous St. Petersburg architect Johann Shedel, the Belfry is an octagon-shaped, four-tiered tower with a gilt cupola. The first tier is built in the style of rustic masonry. The second is decorated with 32 Roman-Doric columns, arranged in groups of four between eight windows. The third is surrounded by 16 Ionic columns in sets of two between eight arches. The third tier housed the tower's 13 bells, the largest of which weighed over 27 tons. Another bell weighing about 16.5 tons was cast in 1732 by the well-known Russian master Ivan Motorin, the author of the "Tsar Bell" in the Moscow Kremlin. Only three small bells have been preserved. The fourth tier of the Belfry is decorated with light Roman Corinthian semicolumns arranged in groups. The 18th-century clock on a special platform of the fourth tier under the cupola was replaced by a new one in 1903, modelled by Moscow artisans after the Kremlin clock. Each

The interior of the St. Sophia Cathedral

The Trinity Gateway Church. 12th-18th centuries

A view of the Vydubechi Monastery and the Bereznyaki housing estate

"The Descent of the Holy Spirit". Detail of the St. Cyril Church paintings by M. Vrubel

The St. Andrew Church. 18th century

quarter of an hour the chimes play a musical scale, and the hours are marked by a corresponding number of bell tolls. The local serf craftsmen Stepan Kovnir, Iosif Rubashevsky, Ivan Gorokh and others took part in the construction of the Belfry.

On the north side of the monastery is the long, 18th-century economic building, where the monastery's economic and administrative offices were located. Beyond it rises the All Saints Church, which was a watch-tower on the wall that girdles the entire territory of the monastery. The All Saints Church is one of the finest examples of the Ukrainian baroque style.

Not far from the remaining part of the Cathedral of the Dormition stands the building which formerly housed the monastery press. Next to it is Kovnir Building. Erected in the 18th century by Stepan Kovnir, it successfully combined the monastery bakery and bookshop, which were put up at different periods. The structure is now a unified architectural whole embellished with pediments. The Kovnir building now houses a museum.

From the viewing platform of the Upper Lavra one can get a good look at the Lower Lavra, whose territory contains caves that have become known as the Near and Far Caves. These ancient caves are first referred to in the *Povesti Vremennykh Let* annals under the year 1051. From the 1060's the churches built aboveground became the centre of the monastery's religious life and the caves turned into a burial site. For nearly six hundred years they served as the monastery cemetery, where the monks, members of the high clergy and feudal princes were interred in special niches, which are marked by tiny windows in the walls of the labyrinths. The caves are the resting place of the chronicler Nestor, the icon-painter Alipi, the physician Agapit and others whose names have come down in history. Specific climatic conditions and the composition of the caves' soil helped mummify the bodies of the dead. The enterprising monks then gave them out to be "sacred relics", created an aura of holiness around the caves and made them into a place of pilgrimage by the faithful. This in turn prompted the clergy to reconstruct the caves from time to time; gradually spacious corridors were built here and the individual side branches were united into a single main circular passageway. Particular importance was attached to the caves' religious decoration: icons and crosses were set up in them and underground churches built, some of which are of high artistic value.

The Far Caves are 280.5 metres and the Near Caves 228 metres long. They lie at a depth of 5 to 15 metres. The corridors are up to 1.5 metres wide and have an average height of two metres. The labyrinths, which are included among the monastery complex of historical monuments, are open to visitors.

The territory of the Kiev-Pechery Museum also includes several museums on the history of art.

The Mariinsky Palace

The monument to Bogdan Khmelnitsky, the outstanding 17th-century general and statesman

THE VYDUBECHI MONASTERY

(A ten minutes' walk along
the Naberezhno-Pecherskaya Road
from the Paton Bridge,
or take trolleybus 15 to the
Botanichesky Sad stop)

The supporting half-arches of the printing house in the Kiev-Pechery Lavra

This group of 11-18th-century architectural monuments lies in a little amphitheatre among the high hills along the Dnieper. Legend has it that it was right across from here that the wooden idol of Perun which was thrown into the Dnieper after the adoption of Christianity was washed ashore. The place's name, Vydubechi, is accordingly derived from the old Russian verb for surfacing, emerging. The monastery itself was founded by Prince Yaroslav the Wise near a crossing over the Dnieper. In 1070 Yaroslav's son Vsevolod laid the foundations here for the Church of St. Michael, one of the outstanding buildings of the time. It was a large, eight-pillared, domed-cross church, richly decorated with frescoes, but only its western part has come down to us. The monastery acquired its present appearance in the late 17th and early 18th centuries with the building of the Cathedral of St. George, an excellent example of a five-cupola, domed-cross church with a cosy refectory and a three-tiered belfry. It is in the Vydubechi Monastery that its Father Superior Silvestr re-edited the ancient *Povesti Vremennykh Let* annals in 1116. The so-called "Kiev Chronicle" was written here.

On the grounds of the Vydubechi Monastery

ASKOLD'S GRAVE
(A ten minutes' walk from the Hotel Dnipro along Petrovskaya Alleya)

According to chronicles and popular tradition, the Princes Askold and Dir became established in Kiev in 862, and that part of the city that had sprung up in the Ugorsk area, in the neighbourhood of present-day Pechersk, began to play the leading role in the life of the city. The Ugorsk area became Askold's fortified residence. It lay farther downstream than the older settlements of Upper Kiev and Podol, in the vicinity of a convenient ford over the Dnieper. Askold evidently regarded this to be of decisive significance for the city's assuming a leading position in the development of commercial ties with the Byzantine empire.

In 882 fighting vessels of the Novgorod Prince Oleg drew up along the bank below Ugorsk. Askold and Dir were killed in the ensuing battle. After becoming master of the city, Oleg moved the princely residence to Starokievskaya (old Kiev) Hill, which most advantageously combined good defence possibilities with proximity to a protected harbour and the main routes connecting the city to the west and south, and declared: "This will be the mother of Russian cities." Oleg laid the groundwork for uniting the East Slav tribes into the single ancient state of Kievan Rus.

In 1810 a church was built according to a design by the well-known architect A. Melensky on the hill overlooking the Dnieper where Askold is said to be buried. The church, a choice specimen of early 19th-century architecture, was later made into a rotonda with a classical colonnade. In 1935 a second storey was added to the building and a park laid around it.

The "Askold's Grave" park

ST. CYRIL CHURCH

(103 Ulitsa Frunze; trolleybus 18)

This fine architectural and artistic monument dates from the 12-19th centuries. In 1146 the Olgovichi princes, who fought long and persistently for the possession of Kiev, founded their own monastery on its northern boundary, where access to the city was most convenient. On a high hill in the centre of the compound they built a monumental stone church dedicated to Saint Cyril. It was a triple-naved, six-pillared domed-cross church with one semispherical cupola. In ancient times it served as a princely sepulchre. One of the heroes of the *Lay of Igor's Host* epic, the Kiev Prince Svyatoslav Vsevolodovich, was interred here in 1194. Up until the mid-17th century, the church and the entire monastery were often subjected to destruction and pillage. The church's appearance was considerably changed as a result of restoration work undertaken in the late 17th and early 18th centuries during which four new octagon cupolas decorated with stucco star-shaped rosettes were added to it. Of particular interest is the church's interior, with its well-preserved monumental wall-paintings—over 800 square metres of 12th-century frescoes, a 17th-century tempera portrait of the monastery's Father Superior and 19th-century oil paintings, among which the compositions of the renowned Russian artist Mikhail Vrubel hold pride of place.

The St. Cyril Church is now a branch of the St. Sophia Museum and houses an exhibition telling about its history, the scholarly research and restoration work that have been done on it and paintings by Vrubel and other 19th-century artists. On Saturdays and Sundays recordings are played here of 16-18th century choral music.

The museum is open from 10 a.m. to 6 p.m. daily except Friday.

The St. Cyril Church. 12th-19th centuries

ST. ANDREW CHURCH

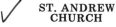

(23 Andreyevsky Spusk; a three minutes' walk from Bogdan Khmelnitsky Square)

For over two centuries now this outstanding creation of the architect Bartolomeo Rastrelli has delighted all who see it with its exquisite forms, majestic design and original location. The distinctive domed-cross five-cupola church (length 32, width 23, and height 42.6 metres, foundation depth up to 15 metres) stands on a steep projection of Starokievskaya Hill, which rises nearly 90 metres above the Dnieper. When you look at it from the streets of the ancient Podol district, it seems to be floating in the air. From

The St. Andrew Church

Vladimirskaya Street lying on a hill, the contours of the church with its Corinthian columns, white pilasters and turquoise and gold cupolas stand out in bold relief against the background of the light-toned expanses beyond the Dnieper.

Rastrelli's design was carried out by his assistant, the Moscow architect I. Michurin. The church's interior is also magnificent, with its fine three-tiered gilt iconostasis, carved ornamentation and sculptures, pulpit and altar canopy. The paintings in the ico-

nostasis were executed by first-rate artists of the time, the Russian A. Antropov and the Ukrainian D. Levitsky. Equally worthy of attention are the paintings "Prince Vladimir Selects a Faith" by an unknown artist and "Apostle Andrew's Sermon on the Banks of the Dnieper" by the local painter G. Borispolets. The church was repaired on several occasions following its consecration in 1767, but did not undergo any substantial alterations. Between 1974 and 1978 it was completely restored, and is now a branch of the St. Sophia Museum. It contains an exhibition devoted to the history of the church and the work of Rastrelli. Here on Saturdays and Sundays one can listen to recordings of 18th-century Russian and Ukrainian choral music.

The museum is open from 10 a.m. to 6 p.m. daily except Thursday.

Tel. 295861

THE MARIINSKY PALACE
(5 Ulitsa Kirova; trolleybus 20, bus 62)

The Mariinsky, or Tsar's, Palace is a fine monument of 18-19th-century architecture, based on a plan by Rastrelli according to which the palace in the village of Perovo near Moscow was also built. Erected in 1755, the Mariinsky Palace with its wings and church premises had a stone first floor and a wooden upper storey, but lost its original appearance during a 1819 fire. It was not until in 1870 that the building was reconstructed. The design by architect K. Mayevsky retained the famous Rastrelli's stylistic peculiarities, and it is in this form that the two-storey baroque stone palace has come down to us. The front façade is 65.3 metres long, the side facing the park—119 metres, the width of the central block is 20 metres and its height—about 16. The palace's paired white semi-columns and turquoise outer walls with their stucco mouldings blend beautifully with the greenery of the adjacent park. The Russian tsars frequently stayed at the Mariinsky Palace and it was the residence of the military governors of Kiev, including the great Russian general Mikhail Kutuzov. In 1917 the revolutionary committee which directed the preparations for the armed October uprising in Kiev had its headquarters in the palace; the Kiev Committee of the Bolshevik Party and the Council of People's Commissars also used the premises for some time following the establishment of Soviet power in the Ukraine. During the years of nazi occupation the Mariinsky Palace was destroyed. After the war it was restored basically to its former state according to a design by the architect P. Alyoshin, and is now protected by the state as an architectural monument. It is the site of official receptions for the city's most honoured guests and of governmental functions on the occasion of important dates and events in the life of the Soviet state.

ST. VLADIMIR CATHEDRAL

**(20 Bulvar Tarasa Shevchenko;
Universitet metro station)**

This functioning church, consecrated in 1896 in honour of the 900th anniversary of Russia's adoption of Christianity is another fine piece of architecture. The first plan of the church, drawn up in 1853 by the St. Petersburg architect I. Shtrom, was not carried out on account of the great construction costs. The foundations for the cathedral were finally laid in 1862 according to Shtrom's design, substantially modified by A. Beretti. Later the prominent Kiev architects R. Berngard, V. Nikolayev and K. Mayevsky and the engineer D. Birkin also took part in its construction. All this led to a certain disharmony in the building's appearance. The triple-naved, eight-pillared, domed-cross cathedral is crowned by seven cupolas and rises to a height of 49 metres. The main façade, which is nearly 30 metres wide, is adorned by a richly ornamented double-leaved doorway with relief bronze sculptures of Princess Olga and Prince Vladimir against a blue enamel background. The cathedral's frescoes were executed by the major Russian artists V. Vasnetsov, M. Vrubel, M. Nesterov, P. Svedomsky, V. Kotarbinsky and others under the direction of Kiev University art professor A. Prakhov.

St. Vladimir Cathedral

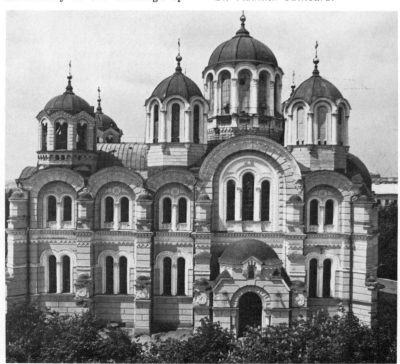

The monument to Prince Vladimir Svyatoslavich (Detail)

THE MONUMENT TO PRINCE VLADIMIR SVYATOSLAVICH

(Vladimirskaya Gorka Park; a five minutes' walk from Ploshchad Leninskovo Komsomola)

The monument to the outstanding statesman of Kievan Rus, Prince Vladimir Svyatoslavich, was unveiled on September 23, 1853. The 20.4-metre-high monument was erected according to a design by the Russian sculptor Vasily Demut-Malinovsky and the architect Konstantin Ton on one of the most picturesque terraces of Vladimir Hill, which towers 70 metres above the Dnieper. The bronze figure of the prince, which is 4.5 metres high and weighs about 6 tons, is the work of professor P. Clodt. St. Vladimir is dressed in the garb of an ancient Russian warrior, with a princely mantle on his shoulders. He holds a large cross in his right hand, and the dynastic Crown of Monomakh in his left. His expressive face is turned toward the mighty Dnieper. The monument's octagonal base, faced in cast-iron slabs, bears the ancient coat-of-arms of Kiev, a bronze bas-relief depicting the Kievans' adoption of Christianity and profuse mouldings of flowers. The monument looks splendid from any angle and adds much to the city's silhouette. It is an important part of the city's architectural and artistic aspect.

THE MONUMENT TO BOGDAN KHMELNITSKY

(Ploshchad Bogdana Khmelnitskovo; trolleybuses 2, 4, 12, buses 20, 38, 68, 71)

The monument to Bogdan Khmelnitsky, a Ukrainian national hero, statesman and military leader, was unveiled on May 15, 1888. It was erected according to a design by the sculptor M. Mikeshin and the architect V. Nikolayev with funds raised by the population. The monument stands on the historic site where the inhabitants of Kiev welcomed

The Monument to Bogdan Khmelnitsky (Detail)

Khmelnitsky after his troops' victory over the Polish invaders. The bronze horseman on the granite pedestal is a most expressive figure: checking his steed in full gallop, Bogdan Khmelnitsky points to the north with his hetman's mace, in the direction of Moscow. This energetic gesture symbolises the Ukrainian people's desire to be forever reunited in a single state with its fraternal Russian people. The monument is one of the city's notable sights.

THE EVER-PRESENT PAST

It is not too long ago that Kiev archeologists finished studying the 5-8th century materials they unearthed during excavations on Zamkovaya, Starokievskaya and Detinseva Hills and in the Podol district. The most important result of these digs was the discovery of an ancient settlement, whose moat and ramparts defended the northeastern projection of Starokievskaya Hill. In it specialists saw actual traits of "Kii town", about which the chronicler Nestor relates the following ancient legend in the *Povesti Vremennykh Let* annals:

"There were three brothers: one was named Kii, the second Shchek, and the third Khoriv, and their sister Lybed. Kii ruled on the hill which is now called Borichev, and Shchek sat on the hill which is now called Shchekovitsa, and Khoriv on the third, which after him was called Khorevitsa, and they founded a city and called it by the name of Kiev (Russian for Kii's.—*Tr.*) in the name of their eldest brother."

There is a legend telling of the visit of Kii, prince of the East Slavs, to Constantinople and his reception there by the Byzantine emperor. Studies of indirect written sources have shown that this visit might have taken place in the

530s, during the reign of the emperor Justinian I. One would naturally expect that Prince Kii set out for Byzantium after his city was founded on Starokievskaya Hill, and materials obtained from archeological digs have confirmed that Kiev arose in the last decades of the 5th century AD. Thus science has thrown new light on the legend and the chronicler's question: "Whence did the Russian land take its origin and who were the first princes in Kiev?" The city of Kiev will mark its 1500th anniversary in May 1982.

Ancient Kiev has given us priceless frescoes, architectural monuments, and a wealth of eloquent museum relics. Many of its street names—Vladimir, Decimal, Golden Gates, Yaroslav's Ramparts, Igor—seem to be taken from the pages of ancient chronicles and together with the very stones of their buildings evoke the images and deeds of distant ancestors—statesmen and simple artisans, brave warriors and talented architects. Everywhere one finds reminders of important dates, striking events, vivid personalities:

—The glorious campaigns of

A view of the Dnieper from Vladimir Hill

the warriors of Prince Oleg, whose rule saw the unification of the ancient Russian lands and Kiev's establishment as the capital city of a mighty state. The princes Igor and Svyatoslav actually put an end to the incessant incursions of nomad tribes.

—In 988 Prince Vladimir Svyatoslavich adopted Christianity and took drastic steps to unite all the Slav principalities into a single state. His possessions stretched from the Baltic and the Carpathians to the Black Sea and the Volga. According to Karl Marx, this period (980-1015) was the "culminating point" in the history of the ancient Russian state, the time of its greatest political might. Kiev became a major centre of commerce, crafts and culture. Its boundaries and population expanded. Extensive construction work went on in the city simultaneously with the erection of new defence works. "Vladimir's Town" became one of the largest and richest cities in Europe.

—After his brilliant victory over the Pechenegs, who had forced their way through to the city, Yaroslav the Wise (1019-1054) erected the new "City of Great Kiev" on the battlesite, to the southwest of "Vladimir's Town". At this time Kievan Rus came to be one of the most powerful states in the world arena. The written language spread, and the city's first cultural and political figures appeared. Foreign merchants and envoys were struck by the luxury and magnificence of

A mosaic on the façade of the Ro-
vesnik Cinema depicting the
founders of Kiev

"Yaroslav's city" with its Golden Gates and St. Sophia Cathedral, the chief metropolitan church of Kievan Rus.

—In the 12th century the chronicler Nestor wrote his immortal *Povesti Vremennykh Let* and an unknown author composed *The Lay of Igor's Host*, that pearl of ancient Russian literature.

...Ancient Kiev went through a period of great flourishing, as well as long years of decline. The feudal division of Kievan Rus into apanage principalities, internecine wars, nomad raids and devastating fires led to the city's loss of its position as the political centre of

Yaroslav the Wise. Stained glass work from the Historical Museum

A reconstructed model of Kiev in the 10th-13th centuries

all Russia, although nominally it remained the state's capital. Its inhabitants had only just managed to raise it from its ruins when the Mongol-Tatar hordes of Khan Batu again razed it to the ground. The charred walls of churches and houses could still be seen in Kiev until the end of the 14th century. A few decades of revival were again followed by a period of desolation after the Crimean Khan Mengli-Girei looted and burnt the city together with its finest monuments in 1482.

Many more foreign conquerors hankered after the keys to Kiev, which are now on display in the historical museum. But the capital city, like the whole of Russia, always fought stubbornly against its invaders.

Kiev played a leading role dur-

The 19th-century keys to the gates of the Kiev-Pechery fortress. Historical Museum

The monument to Grigory Skovoroda, 18th-century Ukrainian educator, philosopher and poet

In the early 18th century this was the study building of the Kiev Academy

ing the Ukraine's war of liberation against its Polish invaders, during its struggle to reunite with Russia. After his victory in the battle of Zholtiye Vody and Korsun, the Hetman Bogdan Khmelnitsky declared Kiev his capital. In January 1654, welcoming the decision of the Pereyaslav Rada (Council on the Ukraine's reunification with Russia, the inhabitants of Kiev took an oath of loyalty to their friendship with the fraternal Russian people.

An active role in the liberation movement was played by the Kiev Brotherhood, a national religious association set up at the Kiev Bratsky Monastery in the Podol district at the beginning of the 17th century. The Brotherhood had a school and was one of the centres of the city's political and cultural life. Its members were Zaporozhye Cossacks headed by the Hetman P. Sagaidachny. In 1632 through the merger of the Kiev Brotherhood and the Kiev Pechery Lavra schools the Kiev-Mogilyansky Collegium was formed. It was transformed into the Kiev Academy by Peter I in 1701. The Academy's graduates included many prominent public leaders and cultural figures who did much to strengthen the ties uniting the Ukrainian, Russian and Byelorussian peoples.

The Ukraine's reunification with Russia had a decisive effect on its economic and cultural development as a whole and that of Kiev in particular. The second half of the 17th and the 18th centuries saw the rebirth of architecture and the growth of national culture and art in the city.

The monument to the outstanding Ukrainian writer Ivan Kotlya-revsky

A plaque commemorating the Decembrists

НА ЦЬОМУ МІСЦІ ЗНАХОДИВСЯ
БУДИНОК, ДЕ В 1822-1825 рр
ВІДБУВАЛИСЯ ТАЄМНІ НАРАДИ
ДЕКАБРИСТІВ

The monument to the great Russian poet Alexander Pushkin

ПУШКІНУ
УКРАЇНСЬКИЙ НАРОД

By the end of the 18th century Kiev already had a population of 30,000. It had considerably grown in area, but in view of its peculiar historical development it lacked territorial integrity and, as in the past, was basically made up of the separate Starokievsky, Pechersk and Podol districts. This period saw the appearance of wooden buildings in the Khreshchataya Valley (present-day Kreshchatik), between whose forest-covered slopes flowed a small stream.

It was only at the beginning of the 19th century that the first draft of Kiev's general development plan was drawn up by the city's chief architect, A. Me-lensky. His plan was in the main implemented in subsequent years.

Between 1806 and 1811 the great Russian general Mikhail Kutuzov was the Governor-General of Kiev. In connection with the Russo-Turkish War, extensive fortification work was carried out in the city under his supervision. Civilian construction was also in full swing: an arcade of shops was begun in the Podol district, and an invalids' home in Pechersk; the candles lighting the city streets were replaced by oil lamps; and the first gymnasium and girls' school were opened in town, as well as a trade school in the Podol

The main block of Taras Shevchenko University

Taras Shevchenko's house-museum

district and several parochial schools.

In the 1820's Kiev became one of the centres of the struggle against the tsarist autocracy by the Decembrists, members of the revolutionary nobility. Congresses of the leaders of their Southern Society, founded in the Ukraine, and talks between representatives of the Southern and Northern societies on a joint armed uprising against tsarism were held in the city. The Decembrists gathered in the Contract House in the Podol district, using the yearly fairs here as a pretext for their coming to Kiev. Another of the Decembrists' frequent meeting-places was the house on Alexandrovskaya Street (presently 14 Kirov St.) belonging

to the hero of the 1812 Patriotic War General N. Raevsky whose family was closely connected with the Decembrist movement. One of the friends of the family was the great Russian poet Alexander Pushkin who had been exiled by the tsarist government to the Ukraine at the time.

After the mid-19th century the city was embellished by many remarkable neo-classical buildings designed by the architects V. and A. Beretti, A. Schille, A. Melensky and others. The most notable of them, which greatly influenced the further development of the city's architecture, was the University building, the work of V. Beretti.

A pleiad of brilliant Russian scientists and cultural figures is linked with Kiev University. Among its honorary members were the scientists Dmitry Mendeleyev, Ilya Mechnikov and Nikolai Pirogov and the writers Ivan Goncharov, Lev Tolstoy, and Ivan Turgenev. The prominent scientists A. Bakh, D. Zabolotny, N. Strazhesko and Y. Tarle, the playwright A. Korneichuk and the poet M. Rylsky studied here at different times.

The magnificent Ukrainian poet, artist and revolutionary and democratic thinker Taras Shevchenko dreamed of teaching at the University. He was taken on here in 1847 as a drawing instructor, but never started work on account of his arrest together with all the other members of the illegal Cyril and Methodius Society,

The early 20th-century building of the former Catholic church

The Polytechnic Institute

Kreshchatik in the latter half of the 19th century

which fought against serfdom. He was banished from Kiev under strict surveillance as a soldier in the Orenburg Corps and prohibited from writing or drawing. The poet loved Kiev and wrote many splendid works there. While in exile he wrote: "...Most often of all I soothe my aged imagination with pictures of gold-domed, garden-cloaked and poplar-crowned Kiev."

Many events in Shevchenko's life and work are connected with Kiev, and its inhabitants lovingly preserve the memory of the great bard. There are now two Shevchenko museums in the city and the University has also been named after him. Across from it, where a statue of Nicholas I once stood, is a monument to the poet.

In second half of the 19th century the first large works of engineering began to appear in the city on the Dnieper. One of them was the suspension bridge over the river, which was built in 1853. Its history is a particle of Kiev's: in 1912 the first electric tram crossed it, in 1920 it was blown up by retreating White Poles, in 1925 it was rebuilt according to a design by the Kiev professor Y. Paton, during the Great Patriotic War it was blown up for the second time, and in 1965 it was replaced by the Metro bridge.

Toward the end of the 19th century the city was becoming a developed industrial centre. By then it had railway connections with Moscow, Kursk and Odessa and its first large industrial enterprises, the present-day Bolshevik and Leninskaya Kuznitsa factories, had sprung up. The first electric station, the first water pipes

Modern buildings on the Dnieper's left bank

and the first electric tram in Russia and second in Europe, which linked Kreshchatik with the Podol district, also made their appearance in Kiev at this time.

In 1898 the first Polytechnic Institute in Russia was founded in Kiev on public initiative and with public funds. The great Russian chemist Dmitry Mendeleyev took an active part in the establishment of this major educational institution.

At the beginning of the 20th century more than half the buildings in Kiev were still wooden; at that time the city's population had already passed the 500,000 mark. As in the other cities of tsarist Russia, only the central part of town was relatively comfortable and well laid out, but the architecture of many public and residential buildings on the city's main thoroughfares, where the local bourgeoisie lived, was characterised by modernistic trends and a mixture of styles.

On the one hand were the fashionable restaurants and stores, banks and rented houses along Kreshchatik street, which became the centre of the city's business life; on the other was the gloomy poverty of the working districts on the outskirts, which had neither water pipes nor sewer systems and where starvation and epidemics took the lives of whole families. These were the faces of Kiev during the rapid development of capitalism in Russia and the Ukraine, in the hard years before the revolution.

On the eve of the First Russian Revolution the city's proletariat already had considerable experience in the class struggle, largely

"The 1905 Sappers' Uprising in Kiev". A drawing on display at the Historical Museum

thanks to the work of Marxist groups, whose active members included the prominent revolutionaries P. Zaporozhets, L. Ketskhoveli, A. Lunacharsky and Y. Melnikov. The Kiev League of Struggle for the Emancipation of the Working Class and the newspaper *Iskra* support-groups played an important part in the working class movement. The Ulyanov family had close connections with the city's Party underground. In 1903-1904 Lenin's mother Maria Alexandrovna and his sisters Anna and Maria lived on Laboratory Street (presently 12 Ulyanovs St.), while his brother Dmitry resided in the centre at what is now 30 Pushkin St. His family kept Vladimir Lenin posted on all the events in the Ukraine's revolutionary struggle.

On October 18, 1905, the blood of the working people was shed on Duma Square (now October Revolution Square) when the police, gendarmes and Cossacks broke up a meeting numbering many thousands, killing and wounding over 500 persons. At the height of the revolutionary movement in the city there arose the Kiev Soviet of Workers' Deputies.

In November 1905 insurgent sappers commanded by second lieutenant B. Zhadanovsky left their barracks arms in hand. Along the way from Pechersk their ranks were joined by workers from the Arsenal and Southern Russian Engineering factory and the Main Railway Workshops, and students. Soldiers and workers, who until then had been on opposite sides of the barricades, marched side by side for the first time. A massacre

The memorial plaque on the wall of the house where Dmitry Ulyanov lived in 1903 and 1904

occurred on Galitskaya Square (now Victory Square), in which hundreds of workers and soldiers were killed and wounded. This insurrection is on a par with the uprising on the battleship *Potemkin*, the revolutionary actions of soldiers and sailors in Sebastopol and other such events.

The heroic traditions of the Kiev proletariat were established in the revolutionary battles of 1905. During the subsequent years of reaction and the First World War it continued to carry on an organised struggle against the autocracy, growing experienced and mature as it prepared for the decisive battles to come. Its traditions manifested themselves to their full extent in October 1917 and January 1918...

The ever-present past... If you gaze carefully at today's city, you will at every step see landmarks from its history.

THE BANNER
OF REVOLUTION

HEROES
OF ARSENAL SQUARE
(Arsenalnaya Metro station)

The streets leading to this small square in the centre of Pechersk District were once the site of selfless fighting by the Kiev proletariat for Soviet power.

On the Moscow Street (Ulitsa Moskovskaya) side, the square is lined by the immense stone wall of one of the shops of the Arsenal Factory, one of the oldest industrial enterprises in Kiev. Pocked with bullet marks, this wall is a silent but eloquent witness to those distant, stormy events.

The victorious October Revolution in Petrograd touched off

"The Arsenal Workers at the Barricades". High relief sculpture

mighty echoes here. On October 29, 1917, the revolutionary Arsenal workers and the soldiers of the Third Airpark formed the vanguard of Kiev's October armed uprising. After three days of stubborn fighting, power came into the hands of the Soviets. But the nationalist bourgeois Central Rada took advantage of this victory to promote its policy of breaking away from Soviet Russia and inciting a fratricidal war. Dealing the insurgents a treacherous blow in the back, the Central Rada established a bloody dictatorship. But in spite of its great losses, the proletariat of Kiev rallied under the leadership of the Bolshevik Revolutionary Committee and prepared for new battles...

In 1923 the cannon from which the Arsenal workers fired the first shot at the troops of the

counter-revolutionary Central Rada was set up on a red granite pedestal in the centre of the square.

In 1961 a high-relief sculpture by M. Korotkevich and N. Kovsun, depicting "The Arsenal Workers at the Barricades", was affixed to the bullet-scarred factory wall, which it was decided to leave untouched. Next to it is the entrance to the People's Museum of the legendary Arsenal factory.

The commemorative plaque on the wall of the house where the Ulyanov family lived

THE MONUMENT TO THE HEROES OF THE GREAT OCTOBER SOCIALIST REVOLUTION

(Sovietskaya Ploshchad; trolleybus 20)

This monument was erected in 1927 over the common grave of the revolutionary workers and soldiers who died the death of the brave in the fighting for Soviet power between October 29 and 31, 1917. Like many others, it was destroyed by the nazi invaders during the last war. It was restored in 1949.

A red granite bowl rests on a black marble slab. The monument's surroundings are equally symbolic: nearby, is the building which served as the headquarters for the Kiev Revolutionary Committee, headed by the ardent Leninist revolutionary A. Ivanov, and the white building of the Ukrainian Supreme Soviet, flying the State Flag of the Ukrainian Soviet Socialist Republic. In the vicinity is a viewing platform with a panorama of today's Kiev.

THE MONUMENT TO THE HEROES OF THE JANUARY ARMED UPRISING

(Sovietski Park; trolleybus 20)

This majestic bronze figure of worker with a banner in his han atop a labradorite pedestal person ifies the fighters who bravel; stood up against the nationalis bourgeois Central Rada in Januar 1918.

...The First All-Ukrainian Cor gress of the Soviets of Worker; and Soldiers' Deputies, held i Kharkov in December 1917, was turning-point in the Kiev proletar iat's struggle for Soviet power The congress proclaimed th Ukraine a Soviet republic and so lemnly declared the establishmen of an indissoluble union betweer the Soviet Ukraine and Sovie Russia.

On the order of the Centra Executive Committee of th Ukraine, revolutionary troops, ac tively supported by units from Soviet Russia, set out from Khar kov onto Kiev shortly after the Congress.

On January 15, 1918, whe the revolutionary troops were al ready approaching the city, a armed uprising began in Kiev under the leadership of the Revo lutionary Committee. As in Oc tober 1917, its focal point was the Arsenal factory; workers from many of the city's districts came to the aid of their Arsenal breth ren. The Central Rada was forced to withdraw its most reliable troops from the front and send them in to suppress the uprising Hard battles were fought for lite-

Heroes of the Arsenal Square

Soviet Square

rally every street. The Arsenal acted as a true bastion in the fighting; its defenders repulsed wave after wave of attacking counter-revolutionaries, their superiors in strength. But their ranks eventually began to thin and their ammunition to run out. On January 21 the blood-thirsty counter-revolutionaries burst onto the territory of the Arsenal factory and massacred the insurgents. Many workers were hacked up and tortured to death on the spot and three hundred were executed by a firing squad.

But the counter-revolutionaries did not enjoy their victory for long. The uprising facilitated the revolutionary troops' successful advance on Kiev. On January 22, Soviet units commanded by Yuri Kotsyubinsky, the son of the outstanding Ukrainian writer Mikhail Kotsyubinsky, occupied the Darnitsa district and the bridges over the Dnieper. Red Cossack detachments commanded by Vitaly Primakov entered the Kurenevka district. There they routed the Central Rada troops, the remnants of which fled. On January 26, 1918, Soviet power was established in Kiev, and on January 30 the entire city turned out for the funeral of the heroes of the January armed uprising.

On Soviet holidays workers with their families use to come to the streets named after the Arsenal heroes Andrei Ivanov, Nikolai Gaitsan, Alexander Anishchenko and Prokop Aistov and lay flowers at the foot of the monuments to their fathers and grandfathers who fought for their future in the revolutionary battles of 1917 and 1918.

The monument to the participants in the January armed uprising of 1918

The monument to the heroes of the January armed uprising was unveiled in 1967.

OCTOBER REVOLUTION SQUARE

(Ploshchad Oktyabrskoi Revolyutsii Metro station)

This square, where the City Duma (assembly) once stood, has witnessed a lot: the flowing blood of workers in 1905, the revolutionary tread of the Red Guard detachments in October 1917, the resounding hoofbeats of the Red Cavalry in January 1918; in November 1943 when Kiev was liberated from the nazis, the Soviet tanks filed by here in a triumphant procession; and it is here that the hitlerites guilty of exterminating thousands of Kiev citizens were executed in accordance with wartime laws as retribution for their butchery.

In 1977 Kiev celebrated the 60th anniversary of the Great October Revolution on the unrecognisably renovated square. It was then that the Monument in Honour of the Great October Socialist Revolution by sculptors V. Borodai, V. Znoba and I. Znoba and architects A. Malinovsky and N. Skibitsky was unveiled.

The monument's red granite pylon in the form of a symbolic unfurled banner, the majestic figure of Lenin and the courageous features of the revolutionary fighters—a worker, a peasant in a soldier's great coat, a woman com-

October Revolution Square during an arts festival

missar and a sailor—look impressive both in the sunny daylight and under their special evening illumination. The glittering streams of the monument's waterfall fountain, the geometric shapes of the flower-beds, which take up an area of 540 square metres, the dark-grey, polished granite slabs which cover its centre, accessible to pedestrians, and the green terraces and steps of its main approach are all conceived in an integral architectural and artistic style.

The monument, which is located in the city centre, is surrounded by the buildings of the October Palace of Culture, the highrise Moskva Hotel, the Tchaikovsky Conservatoire, the Central Post Office and the Ukrainian Trade Union council. The square is, as it were, the heart of Kiev; here one feels with particular intensity the rhythm of this large modern city.

KIEV
IN THE TWENTIETH
CENTURY

In the centre of the capital of the Soviet Ukraine, at the convergence of the city's three main thoroughfares—Kreshchatik, Taras Shevchenko Boulevard (Bulvar Tarasa Shevchenko) and Red Army Street (Ulitsa Krasnoarmeiskaya)—rises a monument to the founder of the Communist Party and the world's first socialist state, Vladimir Ilyich Lenin. The red granite figure of this leader conveys fiery impulse and a passionate appeal to his contemporaries and descendants. Inscribed in gold letters on the statue's pedestal are Lenin's words: "Given united action by the Great-Russian and Ukrainian proletarians, a free Ukraine is *possible*; without such unity, it is out of the question."

The working people of the Ukraine were among those who initiated the formation of the Union of Soviet Socialist Republics in 1922. Under the leadership of the Communist Party and in collaboration with the other peoples of the Soviet Union they successfully coped with the most difficult tasks of socialist industrialisation, collectivisation in agriculture and cultural development and were also able to realise their age-old dream of reuniting all the Ukrainian lands into a single Soviet state.

The Ukraine has become a flourishing republic with a mighty industry, highly developed agriculture and advanced science and culture. It contributes greatly to implementing plans for communist construction in the Soviet Union, to strengthening the unity of the socialist community and developing friendly ties and cooperation among all peoples.

The Ukraine's economy—an integral part of the country's

The monument to Vasily Bozhenko, hero of the 1918-1920 Civil War

single economic complex—is developing according to the laws of socialist division of labour and Lenin's precepts as to the brotherhood of all nations. The Ukrainian people's enormous social and economic achievements have been recorded in its Constitution, which was drawn up with regard to national developmental peculiarities in the letter and spirit of the Fundamental Law of the USSR, the manifesto of a mature socialist society.

...The city on the Dnieper went through a lot during the hard years of the Civil War. Foreign interventionists, White Guard hordes and nationalist bourgeois counter-revolutionaries tried to get a hold on the Ukrainian land and its chief city of Kiev. But underground fighters, led by Communist-Leninists, and workers' detachments defended the gains of Soviet power. Their selfless efforts together with the powerful attacks of the Red cavalrymen led by Vasily Bozhenko, Vitaly Primakov, Nikolai Shchors and Yuri Kotsyubinsky brought the city its long-desired freedom.

...The October Revolution opened up unprecedented possibilities for development to Kiev and all the other cities of the Soviet Union. Planned rehabilitation and construction of residential, public and industrial buildings was begun under socialist conditions. Between 1921 and 1925 alone, 25,000 of Kiev's workers moved into new apartments from the basements and hovels where they used to live.

The 1930s were a time of particularly energetic development for the capital of the Soviet Ukraine. The volume of capital investments in the municipal economy markedly increased and the town's

The monument to Vitaly Primakov, hero of the 1918-1920 Civil War

industrial potential showed rapid growth.

The Soviet people's creative labour was interrupted by the treacherous attack of nazi Germany on the Soviet Union. On June 22, 1941, the first bombs fell on Kiev and many other of the country's towns and villages.

In the very first days of the war, 200,000 of Kiev's inhabitants entered the ranks of the defenders of their socialist homeland. About half the members of the city's Party organisation joined the Red Army. All of Kiev's enterprises were urgently put on a war footing and volunteer corps, communist regiments and avengers' battalions were formed. On July 2, 1941, 160,000 of the city's inhabitants worked on the construction of defence works on the approaches to Kiev.

On July 10 and 11 the front reached the city and its heroic defence lasted for over two and a half months. The nazi command twice issued orders for its troops to parade along Kreshchatik, but their schemes were foiled by the courage of the Soviet soldiers and volunteer corps. The defence of Kiev played an important part in frustrating Hitler's plan for a "Blitzkrieg".

A stubborn struggle against the nazi invaders, in which the Party underground operated with success, began in occupied Kiev. The patriots disrupted all the invaders' attempts to organise the work of the city's enterprises and arrange the supply of their troops.

The enemy marked its stay in Kiev with bloody atrocities. During the years of the city's occupation the nazis tortured, shot, hung and gassed 200,000 of its citizens.

But the hour of liberation came, and on November 6, 1943, the red flag was again raised over Kiev.

The soldiers of the First Ukrainian Front who liberated Kiev found a scene of fearful destruction. Kreshchatik lay in ruins and the city seemed dead. The occupationists had destroyed 42 per cent of Kiev's housing and put more than a thousand of its enterprises out of commission. The city's museum and library collections had been looted and the nazi barbarians had shipped home many artistic treasures from the cathedrals of St. Sophia and the Dormition.

On the day after liberation, the whistle of the Leninskaya Kuznitsa factory sounded over Kiev, and all the remaining enterprises in the city followed its example. Armed with pickaxes and spades, the population began to clear the ruins; they worked over two and a half million man-hours overtime in the ashes of Kreshchatik alone.

The historic Letter of the Working People of the Capital of the Soviet Ukraine to the Russian People, whose text was adopted by the Kievans right after the city's liberation, reads in part: "We publicly confirm that the Ukraine's freedom and happiness lies in its indissoluble union with the Russian people and all the fraternal Soviet peoples. We publicly swear to strengthen this sacred and salutary union. And we bequeath our oath to our children and descendants for all times."

The city's rebirth became the concern of the whole Soviet Union. Machinery and equipment, building materials and provisions reached Kiev day and night from Moscow, Sverdlovsk, Gorky, Tash-

The monument to Vladimir Ilyich Lenin

The monument to the heroic crew of the armoured train Tarashchanets, who were killed in 1919

kent, Ufa and all the fraternal Soviet republics. The solicitude shown by the Communist Party and the state, the collaboration and mutual assistance of all the peoples of the Land of the Soviets and the heroic efforts of the inhabitants of Kiev were the sources of renewal thanks to which the city's grave wounds were quickly healed and it became even richer and more beautiful than before the war.

During the years of postwar construction the city's housing facilities quadrupled and its population more than doubled.

Today Kiev puts out twenty times more industrial produce than before the Great Patriotic War. It makes automatic machine-tools, river boats, excavators, airliners, computer technology, artificial diamonds, motorcycles, television sets, cameras and silk fabrics. The articles its industry manufactures are exported to over sixty countries.

At present there are more than 80 institutions under the Ukrainian Academy of Sciences in Kiev. Science has become an important branch of the Ukrainian capital's economy, in which nearly one out of ten working inhabitants is involved. Particularly productive are the well-known groups of scientists employed at the Yevgeny Paton Electrical Welding Institute, the Cybernetics Institute of the Ukrainian Academy of Sciences, the Institute of Material, and others who do much to accelerate scientific and technological progress.

An unprecedented amount of work has been done in the postwar period to gasify Kiev, develop public transport and the town's park territory. But most impressive of all are perhaps the rate and

The monument to Nikolai Shchors, hero of the 1918-1920 Civil War

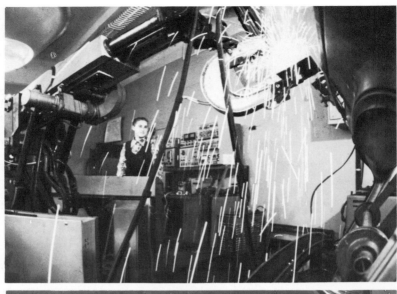

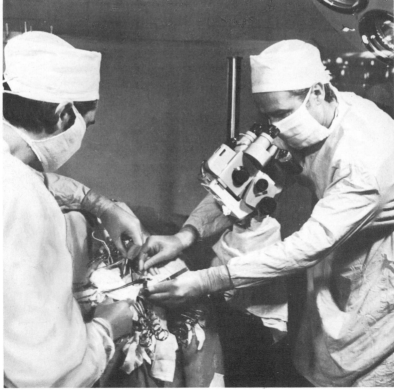

An automatic electric welder of car bodies designed at the Yevgeny Paton Institute

scope of housing construction in the city. During the tenth five-year-plan period alone 6.6 million square metres of housing will have been commissioned in Kiev.

The basic principles of the third Master Plan for the capital of the Soviet Ukraine, which covers the period up to the year 2000, are the even distribution of the population over the city's territory and the combination of urban comfort and natural beauty. The Dnieper with its islets, lakes and coves, which are left untouched in the midst of the new housing developments, is be-

In the operating-theatre of the Institute of Neurosurgery

An atomic reactor at the Nuclear Research Institute

The Moskovsky Bridge built during the ninth five-year-plan period

coming the architectural and compositional pivot of the city's building projects. Bereznyaki, Rusanovka bordered by a man-made canal, Hydropark, Voskresenka, Obolon, Nikolskaya Borshchagovka, Nivki, Vinogradar, Teremki and other new residential districts surround today's Kiev in a white stone ring. Eighty per cent of its present buildings are new.

Every fifteen minutes a baby is born and every twenty minutes a new apartment is finished in Kiev. The comparison is symbolic. Its humane essence is particularly clear if one recalls what an enormous response the Kievans' "All the best for our children! " movement aroused in the republic and the country at large.

In 1976 the City Party Committee, the City Soviet of People's Deputies, the City Trade Union Council and the City YCL Committee drew up a comprehensive

programme of organisational, ideological, educational, social and economic measures to further improve educational, health and other services for children over the 1977-1980 period. By the end of the tenth five-year-plan period about 200 new Young Pioneer camps and clubs for adolescents, 150 school workshops, 19 children's stadiums, five music schools and many other facilities for children will have been built in Kiev.

In the first three years of the tenth five-year-plan period alone oven 100 preschool institutions were built, fifty per cent more than during the entire preceding five-year period. The Kievans' initiative is thus finding actual embodiment.

The city has made great progress in the fields of public education and health protection, which, as everyone knows, are free in the Soviet Union.

Today nearly 200,000 young people are enrolled in Kiev's 18 higher and 40 specialised secondary educational establishments. The material and technical facilities of the hundreds of general education and trade schools, technical colleges and institutes are expanding every year.

Kiev boasts nearly 30,000 medical workers employed in approximately 200 medical, prophylactic and health-building institutions. The municipal health services get scientific and practical help from the city's 22 research organisations. The state allotted 32,000,000 rubles for the construction of medical establishments in Kiev during the tenth five-year period.

Foreign visitors to the city are invariably interested in the basic aspects of the Soviet health care system: prophylaxis, complete checkups of health centres, first aid, etc. The ambulance service of Dijon, France, for instance, is quite aptly named after Kiev, for the Ukrainian capital's experience in organising first aid services has been borrowed here.

In 1958 the first Institute of Gerontology and Experimental Pathology in the Soviet Union and

During the "Days of the Twin-Cities" of Bratislava and Tampere

the world was set up in Kiev. Here a group of scientists from the USSR Academy of Medical Sciences studies the biological foundations of aging and environmental factors that influence longevity. The Institute's policlinic department now keeps tabs on over one hundred Kiev centenarians.

The year 1980 marks two important anniversaries in the life of the Soviet people. Thousands of Kiev's leading workers reached their Tenth Five-Year-plan targets ahead of schedule in honour of the 110th anniversary of the birth of Vladimir Ilyich Lenin and the 35th anniversary of the Soviet people's victory in the Great Patriotic War of 1941-45. At the same time the celebrations provide an opportunity to review the work that the city has done in the last few years. Kiev has built many fine works of engineering and also public buildings. Among them are the new lines of the city's Metro, the large Moskovsky Bridge, the Ukrainian Trade Union Council building, the new

The Economic Achievements Exhibition of the Ukrainian SSR

building of the Kiev branch of the Central Lenin Museum, new cinemas-cum-concert halls, policlinics, schools, sport complexes, libraries and museums.

Kiev's international cultural ties have become varied and intensive in recent years. Days devoted to its twin-cities of Bratislava, Cracow, Leipzig, Kyoto, Tampere, Toulouse and Florence are regularly held in the city. At this time various exhibitions are on display illustrating the development of the twin-cities and the life, work and art of their inhabitants, visiting foreign artists give performances at Kiev theatres and concert halls and the best foreign films are shown in cinemas.

Kievans look to the future with optimism.

A movement with its vanguard of nearly 200,000 Communists in the city Party organisation is presently gathering momentum in Kiev to trasform the Ukrainian capital into a city of highly productive labour, great culture and exemplary public order.

WAR MEMORIALS
IN THE HERO-CITY

THE PARK
OF ETERNAL GLORY
(trolleybus 20)

The memorial complex of the Park of Eternal Glory in honour of the Soviet soldiers who fell during the Great Patriotic War was erected in 1957.

In the centre of the memorial, resting on the edge of a hill overlooking the Dnieper, is the tomb of the unknown soldier. An Eternal Flame burns at the foot of a 26-metre-high granite obelisk, surrounded by a bronze wreath and an abundance of live flowers. Nearby is the necropolis of the heroes who gave their lives for the freedom and independence of their Soviet homeland; the names of 34 fightingmen killed in the battles against the nazi invaders during the defence and liberation of Kiev gleam in the reflection of the Eternal Flame on the marble gravestones. Among those who are buried here are one of the organis-

ers of the city's defence in 1941, Hero of the Soviet Union and commander of the Southwest Front, Colonel-General Mikhail Kirponos, and Hero of the Soviet Union, Sergeant-Major of the Guards Nikifor Sholudenko, whose tank was the first to break through into the burning city on November 6, 1943.

The war brought them together here forever, soldiers, officers and generals, on the banks of the ancient Dnieper in the capital of the Soviet Ukraine. They have now entered the world of legend and become heroes for all time, Captain of the Guards Yuri Novikov and Major-General Anton Pilipenko, Hero of the Soviet Union, Sergeant-Major of the Guards Nikolai Gogichaishvili and Hero of the Soviet Union, Major Ivan Leonov, Colonel Ivan Eliseyev and Major Pyotr Lusta, Hero of the Soviet Union, People's Hero of

The Park of Eternal Glory

The monument to the Hero of the Soviet Union Mikhail Kirponos, one of the commanders in the 1941 defence of Kiev

Komsomol members and Young Pioneers stand in the guard of honour at the heroes' graves, and flowers always lie next to the Eternal Flame.

Here in the Park of Eternal Glory one recalls the fine words of the outstanding Soviet Ukrainian writer and film director Alexander Dovzhenko: "May Kiev never forget the heroes of the Dnieper! May poets sing their glory through the ages over the goodly course of a good many long years, how they ascended Vladimir Hill from all corners of the Soviet Union, how they reddened the white sands of its ancient banks with their blood!"

Yugoslavia Andrei Vitruk and Hero of the Soviet Union, Captain of the Guards Nikolai Avdeyev. The grateful inhabitants of Kiev and the whole Ukrainian people honour the memory of these and many other sons of the multinational Soviet Union.

On national holidays the salvos of military salutes and the anthems of the Soviet Union and the Ukrainian SSR resound in the Park of Eternal Glory and marshals and generals, war veterans and former partisans and underground fighters bow their heads here before the ashes of the dead.

GOLOSEYEVSKY PARK

(trolleybuses 4, 11, 12)

Here on the wooded Goloseyevsky Heights, which occupy key positions on the immediate approaches to the city, the citizens of Kiev first met the enemy, the invading nazi hordes, face to face in July 1941. Volunteer corps fighters and Soviet soldiers engaged in battle here on the defensive lines prepared beforehand by the city's inhabitants, and bitter fighting took place here in August.

The courage of the defenders of Kiev, who fought selflessly on the Goloseyevsky Heights, foiled the enemy's publicly announced intention to hold a parade of the nazi troops on Kreshchatik Street in the presence of the Führer. The Fifth Airborne Brigade under the command of Hero of the Soviet Union Colonel A. Rodimtsev and the Komsomol volunteer regiment particularly distinguished themselves in the battles here. Between August 1 and 16, 1941, over 30,000 of Hitler's soldiers were killed or wounded on the Goloseyevsky lines, and the enemy's frontal attack on the city proved a dismal failure.

On May 8, 1965, when the Soviet people celebrated the twentieth anniversary of their victory in the Great Patriotic War, an Obelisk of Glory was ceremonially unveiled on one of the Goloseyevsky hills. Carved on the red granite rectangle are the words: "This obelisk was erected by the Soviet Ukraine as a token of love, respect and gratitude to you, the Heroes, soldiers and commanders of the Soviet Army, the sailors of the Dnieper military flotilla, the volunteer corps fighters and partisans, who gave their blood and lives in defending Kiev from the nazi hordes between July and September 1941."

The war trenches have long since grown over in the Goloseyevsky forest, and the trunks of trees have closed around the splinters of lethal metal. Properly speaking, this is no longer a forest, but a recreation park. It has been named after the famous Soviet Ukrainian poet and translator Maxim Rylsky, who wrote a cycle of marvellous philosophical and lyrical poems entitled *Goloseyevsky Autumn*. Here in the park is the poet's house, which has now been made into a museum. Nearby are the blocks of the agricultural Academy, the buildings of the Ukrainian Economic Achievements Exhibition and the Kiev centre of international youth tourism "Mir".

Goloseyevsky Park with its picturesque thickets and lakes, numerous entertainment facilities and sports grounds has become a favourite recreation place of the visitors and inhabitants of Kiev alike, the site of art festivals and popular festivities.

There are always many people here, and live flowers surround the Obelisk of Glory at any time of year. Here the Hero City's veterans review the yearly parade of Octobrians, the youngest generation of Soviet patriots, when Victory Day is celebrated in May.

The monument to the workers of Kiev machine-tool plant who were killed at the fronts of the Great Patriotic War

THE MONUMENT TO ARMY GENERAL VATUTIN

(Sovietsky Park; trolleybus 20)

The name of Hero of the Soviet Union, commander of the First Ukrainian Front, Army General Nikolai Vatutin is linked with one of the most impressive pages in the history of the Great Patriotic War, the liberation of the capital of the Soviet Ukraine from the nazi occupationists on November 6, 1943. The battles of Stalingrad and on the Kursk Bulge added to Vatutin's experience in military command, which he brilliantly applied in the battle for the Dnieper.

Before advancing on Kiev, where Vatutin had studied and worked until the war, the commander of the Front said at a meeting in his headquarters: "The Hitlerites try to frighten us by claiming they have bound the Dnieper in concrete and iron and turned it into an inaccessible 'Eastern Rampart'. But we are convinced that our valorous soldiers will force the river on their first attempt and seize the bridgeheads on the right bank. We have been accounted the great honour of liberating the capital of the Soviet Ukraine from nazi servitude. Kiev awaits us, comrades! "

The course of the offensive operation confirmed these words of his. Masterfully executing a daring manoeuvre, the soldiers of the First Ukrainian Front forced the Desna and the Dnieper in a lightning spurt, overcame the enemy's fierce resistance in street fighting and took the city by storm. The red flag was raised over the building of the Central Committee of the Ukrainian Communist Party at 12:30 a.m. on November 6, 1943, and Kiev became Soviet once again on the eve of the 26th anniversary of the Great October Revolution.

At a city-wide meeting on November 27, 1943, General Va-

tutin addressed the following words to the citizens of Kiev: "We know what bleak days of privation and grief you had to endure during these two years. But the Soviet people have never submitted to anyone, nor will they ever. Glory to the heroes of the Battle of Kiev! The hour of our victory is near! "

About 2,500 officers and soldiers were awarded the high title of Hero of the Soviet Union for the forcing of the Dnieper and liberation of Kiev, and thousands received Orders and medals. Among them were representatives of almost all the nationalities and peoples of the Soviet Union and soldiers in the First Czechoslovak Independent Brigade commanded by Ludvik Svoboda. Sixty-five Red Army units and formations were given the honorary appellation of "Kiev".

"To Hero of the Soviet Union General Vatutin from the Ukrainian people" is inscribed in gold on the pedestal of the monument erected on the commander's grave in 1947.

The Soviet general Nikolai Vatutin died in Kiev on April 15, 1944, after being gravely wounded.

The granite statue of the hero is the work of the well-known Soviet sculptor Yevgeny Vuchetich.

The bas-reliefs on the monument to General Nikolai Vatutin

The memorial honouring the soldiers of the First Czechoslovak Independent Brigade who took part in the liberation of Kiev in 1943

THE MONUMENT
TO THE TANK CREWS
WHO TOOK PART IN
THE LIBERATION OF KIEV

(Zavod Bolshevik Metro station)

The monument was unveiled on November 3, 1968, as a token of the people of Kiev's eternal gratitude to the Guards of the Third Tank Army, who liberated the city from the nazi invaders.

...On a November night in 1943 when a crimson glow blazed over Kiev, a Guards tank company with a landing party of sub-machine gunners burst through here in the area of Brest-Litovsk Avenue (Brest-Litovsky Prospekt) to head off the retreating nazi forces. A Battle ensued in the course of which the commander's T-34 tank was put out of action but its crew continued to fight, knocking out three enemy tanks and devastating a column of enemy vehicles...

One of the famous T-34 tanks, a fighting machine of legendary fame which inspired terror in the nazis, has now been erected on a pedestal in memory of the exploits not only of the heroes of the battle front but also of the heroes of the home, the workers, engineers and scientists from all the fraternal Soviet republics who tirelessly forged this victorious

The monument to the Soviet civilians and war-prisoners who were murdered in 1941-1943

The Eternal Flame

The Obelisk of Glory honouring the participants in Kiev's heroic defence of July-September 1941

The Mound of Immortality, a monument to those who fell in the Great Patriotic War

The monument to Hero of the Soviet Union, General Nikolai Vatutin

The monument to the heroic Soviet tank crews who took part in the 1943 Battle for Kiev

weapon. A group of Ukrainian automatic welding experts headed by the outstanding scientist Yevgeny Paton, who were evacuated from Kiev to the Urals in 1941, did much to make the armour-plating on Soviet tanks invulnerable. The so-called "Paton seam" proved its worth in all the major tank engagements of the Great Patriotic War.

THE MOUND OF IMMORTALITY

(Park Pobedy; a ten minutes' walk from the Darnitsa Metro station)

This distinctive memorial to those who fell in the Great Patriotic War was opened on June 21, 1967, in the centre of the new Victory Park, laid out by the inhabitants of Kiev together with envoys from the Hero Cities of Moscow, Leningrad, Odessa, Sebastopol and Volgograd.

The Mound contains earth brought here from the soldiers' graves in many villages and towns of Russia, the Ukraine and Byelorussia.

A broad avenue leads up to the Mound of Immortality, built in the shape of a relief five-pointed star whose contours are delimited by granite blocks. The star is always radiant with live flowers.

The museum dedicated to Kiev's liberation from the nazi invaders in 1943

THE MEMORIAL COMPLEX DEDICATED TO THE 68,000 VICTIMS OF NAZISM

(Darnitsa Woods; special bus)

Sixty-eight thousand Soviet civilians, soldiers and officers were tortured to death by the nazis between 1941 and 1943 in the Darnitsa concentration camp. The present memorial complex was opened on the site of the former death camp on November 3, 1968.

The entrance to the memorial symbolically incorporates part of the barbed-wire and chain-link fence which once surrounded the territory of the camp. The avenue leading to the complex's main monument is covered with granite slabs. A stone lying at its edge bears the inscription: "The martyrs' last path. Exhausted, famished and bloody, they walked

The monument of the Soviet civilians and war-prisoners who were tortured to death by the nazis in the Darnitsa concentration camp

The monument to the Polytechnic Institute's students and teachers who were killed during the Great Patriotic War

his trail to be shot, carrying in heir hearts hatred for the enemy nd faith in our victory."

At the end of the avenue in the nidst of a small clearing surround-d by pines, is a hill whose top is rowned by a granite sculpture epicting a group of uncowed oviet soldiers supporting one nother. The epitaph on the near-y tombstone calls on the living) remember the tragedy of the. ast war.

BABI YAR
(Ulitsa Demyana Korotchenko; trolleybus 16)

The whole world knows of the tragedy of Babi Yar, like that of Khatyn, Lidice and Oswiecim. Here the nazis committed one of their most bestial crimes.

The occupation of Kiev lasted 779 days, throughout which period mass executions went on in Babi Yar. The nazi invaders merci-lessly exterminated members of the Soviet underground and parti-sans, captured Soviet soldiers and officers, as well as thousands of civilians, among them many chil-dren, women and old people.

The monument which rises over the former Babi Yar in the park of the Syrets housing estate serves as an eternal reminder of this tragedy. The inscription on it reads: "Over ONE HUNDRED THOUSAND citizens of Kiev and prisoners-of-war were shot here by the nazi invaders between 1941 and 1943."

The monument's composition symbolises the courage and unbroken spirit of the Soviet people. The central avenue leads up to a raised platform on which eleven bronze figures stand arrested in motion. In front is a Communist member of the underground, boldly looking death in the face with eyes filled with resoluteness and confidence in the triumph of the just cause. A soldier stands with tightly clenched fists next to a sailor shielding an old woman. A young boy who refused to bow his head before the nazis falls into the death pit. Crowning the group is the figure of a young mother, a symbol of life's triumph over death.

The monument to the Soviet civilians and war prisoners who died at the hands of the nazis in Babi Yar

The monitor *Zheleznyakov, a monument to the sailors of the Dnieper flotilla who displayed heroism during the Great Patriotic War*

THE MONUMENT TO THE BRAVE FOOTBALLERS OF THE KIEV DYNAMO TEAM

(Dynamo Stadium; a three minutes' walk from the Hotel Dnipro)

The exploit of the Kiev footballers who were shot by the nazis has been immortalised in a monument unveiled at the Dynamo Stadium on June 19, 1971.

...One of the Dynamo soccer team's favourite players, Makar Goncharenko, was wounded in the fighting in the Goloseyevsky forest during the city's defence and thus ended up on occupied territory. On learning that besides Goncharenko a few more of the famous Kiev Dynamo players were left in the city, the nazis decided to arrange a match be-

The monument to the Kiev Dynamo footballers who were shot by the nazis

tween them and the Luftwaffe team, one of their army's best, which included professional players.

"We well realised," reminisced Goncharenko, one of the participants in the "death match", "that this would be no simple match. They tried to intimidate us by warning that we'd be hung on the goal if we won. The referee entered the dressing-room before the start of the game. He was dressed not in traditional garb, but in Gestapo uniform. He ordered: 'We have a single greeting—Heil Hit-ler! Don't you forget it.' The teams drew up in the centre of the field. The Germans raised their arms in their habitual salute. Our lads thrice gave the traditional cry of Soviet players. This was already a direct manifestation, but for the time being it, as well as our red football jerseys, were forgiven, for everything would be settled during the game. The match got off to a difficult start. The Luftwaffe players knew that we, emaciated and famished, had little strength, and had not trained for a long time to boot. The first half ended

with the Germans leading by a score of 3:2. We conferred during the break. The referee wouldn't let us get anywhere near the penalty area: he declared it to be 'offside', and that was that. We knew we could expect reprisals if we won. But we had to win without fail. So we'd shoot for the goal from a distance. That's what we decided, and that's how we began the second half."

The Dynamo team won that memorable game with a score of 5:3. One of the goals was made by Goncharenko. The enraged nazis threw the Kiev players into a concentration camp, where Goncharenko was able to escape death only by a miracle.

...The 4.3-metre-high monument is situated near the entrance to the stadium's stands. The figures of the courageous participants in the "death match" who were executed by the Hitlerites, Ivan Kuzmenko, Nikolai Trusevich, Alexei Klimenko and Nikolai Korotkikh, seem to rise out of the mighty granite block. The monument is surrounded by a green lawn suggesting a soccer field, and four birches.

THE SEASONS IN KIEV

The city on the Dnieper is beautiful at any time of the year. In spring it is filled with a riot of chestnut blossoms, in summertime its streets and squares are shaded by the thick green crowns of trees. Autumn decks parks and gardens in a captivating array of crimsons and golds, which in winter give way to the lacy white patterns of hoar-frost and snow.

Kiev has a mild, moderate continental climate. The average yearly temperature of the air is +7.2ºC. The average temperature of the warmest month, July, is +19.5°C, while that of the coldest, January, is —5.8°C. On the hottest days of the year the thermometer can rise to +40°C, and on the coldest it may drop to —34ºC. An average 600 mm of precipitation a year falls in the Kiev region, but the amount can exceed 900 mm.

In May the city celebrates the "Kiev Spring" arts festival, when companies from all the fraternal Soviet republics perform on the stages of theatres and Palaces of Culture, in the parks or simply in the street, and Kiev becomes filled with multilingual speech, a polyphony of music and a colourful assemblage of national costumes.

The summer is the peak of the tourist season, a time of mass recreation along the Dnieper, of tours by theatre and variety groups from other republics of the Soviet Union and many foreign countries.

Kiev is resplendent in autumn, with bunches of flaming rowanberries hanging from the branches of still leafy trees and masses of shiny brown chestnuts.

In winter Kiev's streets and parks are covered with a soft layer of snow, the ice-hummocks on the Dnieper sparkle in the sun and

The Ukraina Palace of Culture

The "Kiev Spring" arts festival

thousands of lovers of ice fishing patiently sit by holes in the river's frozen surface. The Ice Stadium is the site of exciting sports encounters, and the air is filled with the ringing of troika bells and the delicious smell of *blini* during the traditional "Goloseyevskaya Shrovetide" holiday.

Modern-day Kiev covers an area of over 80,000 hectares, more than half of which is taken up by woods, public gardens, parks and tree-lined boulevards. There is about 20 square metres of greenery for each inhabitant, much more than in many European capitals. Kiev is justly called one of the world's greenest cities, with its 66 parks, 39 boulevards and more than 170 public gardens. To this must be added its three wooded parks, which embrace 38 mass recreation zones. These scenic spots draw campers and groups of relaxing Kievans and tourists.

The capital's green zone is an object of particular concern and pride on the part of its inhabitants. Back in 1937, a scientifically-grounded verdurization programme was elaborated in Kiev. It provided for the formation of a system of parks and gardens embracing absolutely all the city's districts, their even distribution over its entire territory and func-

Taras Shevchenko Boulevard

tional differentiation (health-building, mass recreation, sports and other areas), the transformation of forests into wooded parks and the creation of a closed outer ring of forests and an inner ring of parks around the core of the city.

The programme began to be carried out mainly after the war when the Victory, Peoples' Friendship, Partisan Glory, Grushki and International parks were formed. The largest of them is the Peoples' Friendship Park, with an area of 520 hectares. It was laid out on the left bank of the Dnieper in 1972, in honour of the 50th anniversary of the formation of the Union of Soviet Socialist Republics, and successfully combines cultivated landscapes and expanses of virgin nature. In the near future two more parks of

The fountain in the Golden Gates garden

A road junction in the Nikolskaya Borshchagovka housing estate ▶

The Dnieper's embankment in summer

The Dnieper on a calm day

Spring comes to Kiev

In the Golo-seyevsky Park

The Mlyn Restaurant in the Hydropark

Environmental protection is a particular concern of Kievans

The bridge over the Venetsiansky strait in the Hydropark

approximately the same size will appear on the left bank of the Desenka next to the Troeshchina residential district and on the right bank of the Dnieper near the Obolon housing estate.

All the old parks along the high right bank of the Dnieper—the Vladimir Hill, Young Pioneer, First of May and Soviet parks—as well as the green slopes of the Dnieper and Askold's Grave, have merged into the Central Recreation Park, which has an area of over 260 hectares. Much work has been done to improve the park, including the laying of a road which links Petrovskaya Avenue (Petrovskaya Alleya) with the Dnieper Descent (Dneprovsky Spusk), Park of Eternal Glory and Embankment Highway (Naberezhnoe Shosse). Imposing historical and cultural monuments, viewing and concert platforms, amusement parks and pavilions, cinemas, restaurants and cafés are to be found on the Central Park's

picturesque terraces. Adjoining the Park Road is 4,000-seat open-air theatre (Zelyony Teatr), which harmoniously blends in with the surrounding terrain, stands of greenery, the remains of an ancient bastion of the Pechersk fortress and park architecture elements.

The Fiftieth Anniversary of the October Revolution Park, laid on the territory of a former settlement which was destroyed during the war, is very **popular** among Kiev's inhabitants. It lies on an island washed by the waters of the Dnieper and the Venetsiansky (Venetian) and Rusanovka straits and is connected with the city by a Metro line. Avenues lead from the Metro station to the beaches and recreation areas. The city's Master Plan provides for the creation of three zones in this 260-hectare hydropark: a zone of cultural and sports facilities, an amusement-park zone and a mass recreation zone. Cafés, a restau-

Relaxing on the Dnieper

The traditional "Farewell Winter" festival

The Vitaly Primakov Park in autumn

A winter park

rant and vending stands have been built here.

Kiev's system of verdant zones begins in the forests of Kiev Region and forms a nearly uninterrupted circular belt of protective wooded parks along the city boundaries. It extends in wedges into the built-up areas of town and merges with the green expanses of local parks, gardens and boulevards. Green zones break up Kiev's territory into separate districts. By late 1980 the amount of verdure in the city will have nearly doubled and there will consequently be 38 square metres of greenery for every inhabitant.

Much attention is also devoted in Kiev to protecting the city's air and water. No new enterprises are planned within the city limits, except for those essential to satisfy the population's needs. During the last few years about 60 per cent of the city's industrial enterprises and workshops have been moved outside its boundaries.

Suburban health resort zones superbly complement the city centre's water and park preserves. Such places as Pushcha-Voditsa, Koncha-Zaspa and Vorzel, which have a great number of health and holiday homes, are famous for their salubrious forests and air, ponds and lakes.

The protection of Kiev's environment is a matter of both state and public concern. This is why Kiev now has an integral area of greenery, which makes for healthy natural surroundings for its inhabitants and a unique architectural landscape; this, too, is why it is beautiful in all seasons.

CULTURAL TREASURES

Kiev is one of the Soviet Union's major cultural centres. Statistics show that every evening upwards of 5,000 persons attend the city's seven theatres (three of which have the high title of Academic), nearly 50,000 persons fill the premises of its 116 Palaces and Houses of Culture and clubs, and 115,000 persons go to its 77 cinemas. (Open to Kievans and visitors to the city are a large number of state museums and about 1,300 libraries with a total collection of 65,000,000 books. More than 110,000 Kiev working people are members of amateur art groups of various kinds.

The city's museum collections are rich and varied. The *Kiev Branch of the Central Lenin Museum* (57 Vladimirskaya Ulitsa; tel. 240291; closed Monday) is a major centre for popularising the ideas of Marxism-Leninism. The museum's more than 7,000 exhibits tell not only of the life and activities of the great Lenin, but also of the history of the Party he founded, the heroic accomplishments of the Soviet people, the development of the world communist and national liberation movement, the struggle of the world's peoples for peace, democracy and socialism and the ultimate triumph of the immortal ideas of Marxism-Leninism.

The *Ukrainian Museum of the History of the Great Patriotic War of 1941-1945* (8 Ulitsa Chekistov; tel. 936071; closed Monday) was opened in 1974 to perpetuate the memory of the Soviet people's feat of arms. Its 20 rooms hold

The Lenin Museum

more than 6,000 exhibits, including the battle standards of military units and partisan detachments, photographs and personal effects of Soviet Army soldiers and officers and specimens of the weapons used. In chronological order the displays describe how the Soviet people, led by the Communist Party, won a victory of worldwide historic importance over nazism, defended the freedom and independence of its socialist homeland and saved the peoples of Europe from enslavement.

The *Historical Museum of the Ukrainian SSR* (2, Vladimirskaya Ulitsa; tel. 294864; closed Monday) has a fund of over 450,000 items exhibited over an area of 32,000 square metres. During the years of Soviet power the museum has become a real treasury of historical relics. Visitors are inva-

riably attracted to its dioramas of "The Heroic January 1918 Uprising of Kiev's Workers and Soldiers", "The Storming of the Perekop Isthmus", "The Construction of the Dnieper Hydroelectric Power Station", "Ancient Kiev", "The Fraternal Meeting of the Don and Zaporozhye Cossacks" and so on.

The *Museum of Historical Treasures of the Ukrainian SSR* (21 Ulitsa Yanvarskovo Vosstaniya; tel. 976032; closed Tuesday) is a branch of the Historical Museum. It is housed in nine rooms of a building erected in the 18th century by the talented Ukrainian serf architect Stepan Kovnir. The museum has a unique collection of artifacts dating from the 6th century BC to the 19th century

The Museum of the Great Patriotic War of 1941-1945

AD. Among the items on display are many highly artistic platinum, gold and silver objects decorated with precious stones, and the famous gold pectoral ornament of a Scythian ruler, a priceless find by Ukrainian archeologists. There are also collections of West European and Russian medals, and. Ancient Greek, Roman, Byzantine, Polish, Austrian, Italian, Spanish, French, German, Dutch, English, American, Chinese, Japanese and Egyptian coins.

The *Ukrainian Fine Arts Museum* (6 Ulitsa Kirova; tel. 296462; closed Friday) is one of Kiev's leading art museums. It has some of the finest examples of Ukrainian painting, sculpture, drawings and other fine arts from the 12th century to the present, split into two sections covering the pre-revolutionary and Soviet periods.

The *State Museum of Decorative Ukrainian Folk Arts* (21 Ulitsa Yanvarskovo Vosstaniya; tel. 976540; closed Tuesday) was opened in 1954. It has over 50,000 unique specimens of folk art from the 15th century to the present—wood carvings, fine embroidery, weaving, ceramics, clothing, glass, porcelain and pottery.

There are about 200,000 exhibits in the repositories of the

The open-air exhibition grounds of the Museum of the Great Patriotic War

Museum of Theatrical, Musical and Film Arts of the Ukrainian SSR (21 Ulitsa Yanvarskovo Vosstaniya; tel. 977652; closed Tuesday), among which are the manuscripts of prominent artistic figures, photographic materials, posters, programmes, scores, costumes, props, sketches of sets and trappings by outstanding theatre artists, and paintings, sculptures and drawings.

Many of the exhibits at the *Kiev Museum of Russian Art* (9 Ulitsa Repina; tel. 246107; closed Thursday) testify to the strong links between Ukrainian and Russian culture. The museum has 35 rooms whose displays of paintings by outstanding Russian artists of the past and present reflect the basic stages in the development of Russian art from the 12th century to the present.

The works of the finest foreign artists are assembled at the *Kiev Museum of Western and Eastern*

The Historical Museum of the Ukrainian SSR

A room in the Historical Museum of the Ukrainian SSR ▶

Art (15 Ulitsa Repina; tel. 246162; closed Wednesday). The origins of the museum's collections date back to the late 1870's, when the local connoisseurs of Western and Eastern art B. and V. Khanenko began to buy outstanding works in Paris, Rome, Florence, Berlin, Vienna and Warsaw and at antique fairs in Moscow, St. Petersburg and Kiev. As a result they amassed a valuable collection of West European paintings and sculptures, antique sculptures, terracotta and glass, Italian majolica, antique furniture, tapestries, enamels, silver, coins, fabrics and works of Eastern art. These formed the basis for the museum, which was founded in 1919, and it has become a true treasure-house of art.

The *Taras Shevchenko Museum* (12 Bulvar Tarasa Shevchenko;

Detail of the pectoral ornamen on display at the Museum o, Historical Treasures of the Ukrai nian SSR

The Ukrainian Fine Arts Museum

tel. 242523; closed Monday) is very popular among both residents of Kiev and visitors. Its 24 rooms contain documents relating to the life and work of the great Ukrainian poet, manuscripts of his works, rare photographs, lifetime and nearly all succeeding editions of his works and original paintings and drawings.

There is a large collection of materials dealing with the poet's life in Kiev at the *Taras Shevchenko Literary and Memorial House-Museum* (8a Pereulok Tarasa Shevchenko; tel. 293511; closed Friday).

Lovers of books and students of their history might like to visit the *State Museum of Books and Printing of the Ukrainian SSR* (21 Ulitsa Yanvarskovo Vosstaniya; tel. 976449; closed Tuesday), located in Kiev's first printing house, which was founded in 1615. Its over 3,000 exhibits trace the origins of the Slavs' written language, the appearance of the first manuscript books, the development of printing in the Ukraine since its inception and the establishment and flowering of Soviet publishing.

The following museums are also of interest:

The *"Kosoi kaponir" historical, revolutionary and architectural monument and museum* (24

Gospitalnaya Ulitsa; tel. 675791; closed Monday);

The *Museum of Folk Arhitecture and Ethnography of the Ukrainian SSR* (Pirogovo Village; tel. 662406; closed Wednesday);

The *Literary-Memorial Museum of the Ukrainian poetess Lesya Ukrainka* (97 Ulitsa Saksaganskovo; tel. 214235; closed Thursday);

The *Literary-Museum of the Ukrainian poet Maxim Rylsky* (7 Ulitsa Maksima Rylskovo, tel. 631210; closed Friday);

The *Literary-Memorial House-Museum of the Ukrainian Playwright Alexander Korneichuk* (Plyuty Village; tel. 614358; closed Monday);

The *Central Natural History Museum of the Ukrainian Aca-*

N. Burachek. "The Road to the Collective Farm". The Museum of Ukrainian Fine Arts

The Museum of Russian Art

Exhibits from the Museum of Decorative Ukrainian Folk Art

The Museum of Folk Architecture and Ethnography of the Ukrainian SSR

Madonna and Child by G. Bellini at the Museum of Western and Eastern Art

The Taras Shevchenko Opera and Ballet Theatre

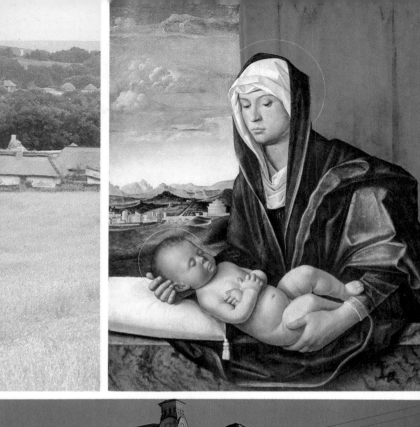

The Ivan Franko Ukrainian Drama Theatre

In the opera studio of the Tchaikovsky Conservatoire

At the Museum of Books and Printing of the Ukrainian SSR

demy of Sciences (15 Ulitsa Lenina; closed Wednesday);

The *Central Literary and Art Archives Museum of the Ukrainian SSR* (22a Ulitsa Vladimirskaya; tel. 294481; closed Saturday and Sunday).

The *Taras Shevchenko Opera and Ballet Theatre of the Ukrainian SSR* (50 Vladimirskaya Ulitsa; tel. 247144, 245509) occupies a leading place in the Ukrainian capital's theatrical life. During its history of more than a century the theatre has witnessed vivid episodes in the struggle of progressive cultural figures for a democratic art. In their day the world-famous Fyodor Chaliapin, Leonid Sobinov, Antonina Nezhdanova and Valeria Barsova sang here, as did Ukrainian operatic stars Maria Litvinenko-Volgemut and Ivan Patorzhinsky. The

The monument to the outstanding Ukrainian poetess Lesya Ukrainka

The monument to the great Ukrainian writer Ivan Franko

theatre's present company, which includes the invariably popular singers People's Artists of the USSR Yevgenia Miroshnichenko, Dmitry Gnatyuk, Anatoly Mokrenko and Anatoly Solovyanenko and many brilliant ballet dancers is also widely known. The Kiev productions of Y. Meitus's opera "The Young Guard", K. Dankevich's "Bogdan Khmelnitsky", G. Maiboroda's "Milana" and "Arsenal", M. Skorulsky's ballet "Forest Song" and many others became landmarks in the development of Ukrainian musical theatre art. Productions of Russian and Ukrainian classics are a popular part of the theatre's repertoire. For its outstanding services in developing culture and art, the theatre has been awarded the Order of Lenin and of the Red Banner of Labour.

The *Ukrainian Theatre* (3 Ploshchad Ivana Franko; tel. 29591) bears the name of the celebrated Ukrainian writer Ivan Franko. It has staged nearly all the works of the Soviet Ukrainian dramatist Alexander Korneichuk and its current repertoire includes Ukrainian, Russian and foreign classical and modern plays.

The *Russian Drama Theatre*, named after the Ukrainian poetess Lesya Ukrainka, (5 Ulitsa Lenina; tel. 249063) is the city's oldest company. It often puts on the best plays from the fraternal Soviet republics and abroad, and its stagings of plays by Pushkin, Ostrovsky, Gorky, Naidyonov, Chekhov, Tolstoy, Trenyov, Ivanov, Pogodin and Lavrenyov have been notable events in Kiev's theatrical life.

Boxes at the Opera and Ballet Theatre

The Kiev ballet is applauded all over the world

You might also like to see:

The *Operette Theatre* (53/3 Krasnoarmeiskaya Ulitsa; tel. 272241);

The *Leninist Komsomol Theatre for Young Spectators* (15/17 Ulitsa Rozy Luxembourg; tel. 935475);

The *Puppet Theatre* (13 Ulitsa Shota Rustaveli; tel. 251059);

The *Kiev State Philharmonic Society* (2 Vladimirsky Spusk; tel. 296251);

The *Opera Studio of the Tchaikovsky Conservatoire* (11 Ulitsa Kreshchatik; tel. 291242);

The *Circus* (1 Ploshchad Pobedy; tel. 740120);

The *Ukraina Palace of Culture* (103 Krasnoarmeiskaya Ulitsa; tel. 683308);

The *Oktyabrsky Palace of Culture* (1 Ulitsa Oktyabrskoi Revolyutsii; tel. 297492).

A show of the Kiev Music Hall

The Operetta Theatre

For information on the current work and plans of members of Kiev's intelligentsia visit:

The *Club of the Ukrainian Writers' Union* (2 Ulitsa Ordzhonikidze; tel. 934586);

The *Artists' Club* (1-5 Ulitsa Artyoma; tel. 791481);

The *Cinema Club* (6 Ulitsa Saksaganskovo; tel. 275225);

The *Architects' Club* (7 Novopushkinskaya Ulitsa; tel. 249227);

The *Actors' Club* (13 Ulitsa Shota Rustaveli; tel. 251069);

The *Scientists' Club* (45 Vladimirskaya Ulitsa; tel. 244236).

SPORTING KIEV

A P.E. class in a kindergarten

Olympic champion sprinter Valery Borzov

Prominent figure-skaters Irina Moiseyeva and Andrei Minenkov performing in Kiev

A rhythmic gymnastics class at a sports school

The Sports Palace

Every fourth inhabitant of this city of more than two million people regularly engages in some form of sport or physical fitness activity. They are able to pursue their sporting hobbies in the city's 830 physical fitness groups set up at factories, building sites, educational and other establishments. These groups are affiliated to sports societies and organisations.

Physical fitness activities are usually best organised in those establishments where the managers themselves regularly engage in sport. For example, Academician Boris Paton, President of the Ukrainian Academy of Sciences; general aircraft designer Oleg Antonov; Victor Glushkov, director of the Institute of Cybernetics of the Ukrainian Academy of Sciences to name but a few, are all enthusiastic sportsmen.

Every four years USSR Games are held, and as part of this Kiev also holds its own city games. The 1978 Kiev Games involved the participation of more than 800,000 people, with contests in nearly 40 different sports.

Close attention is given in Kiev to the task of ensuring the fitness of the population. More than 200 sports grounds have been laid in residential areas, particularly in the new estates. Every year multisport competitions are held: the Youth Games for children and teenagers, and the Health Games for adults. The highlights of these are the football and ice-hockey contests held in the residential areas.

Emphasis is also placed here on the development of sport for children. Right from infancy children are placed under the su-

A bird's-eye view of the Central Stadium

pervision of doctors and sports consultants. The majority of the city's tots attend pre-school establishments where physical education is a high priority and is directed towards the child's all-round development, and improving its fitness. In these establishments children are taught to swim, ski, skate and ride a bicycle.

An important stage in children's physical education begins at school. At present there are more than 50 sports schools in the city, providing coaching for more than 20,000 boys and girls. The curricula of general schools make provisions for compulsory gym classes, athletics and other sports.

A total of almost 3,000 full-time P.E. teachers are employed in Kiev to further the development of physical education and sport amongst the city's inhabitants.

Kiev has impressive material and technical facilities for the development of physical fitness activities and sport, including 21 stadiums, 22 swimming pools, 420 gymnasiums, an indoor athletics arena, an ice stadium, a Palace of Sports and thousands of playgrounds. Coming years will see a notable increase in the number of such sports facilities. Funds for their construction are allocated not only by the state, but also by trade unions, enterprises and establishments.

All this taken together constitutes a firm foundation for the development of sport. In 1978 alone 17 residents of Kiev won the title of world champion, 25 that of European champion, 80 that of USSR champion, and 71 became Masters of Sport (international

Kiev fans

Merited Masters of Sport of the USSR, world, European and USSR champions Nadezhda Tishchenko and Margarita Kukharenko

class), all of whom form part of the city's pool of potential Olympic material.

The Soviet Union's first Olympic team, which took part in the Helsinki Games in 1952, included 13 residents of Kiev. The first of our citizens to win an Olympic gold was the gymnast Nina Bocharova.

Citizens of Kiev were prominent in all the following Olympics, and their representation in the national team constantly grew in size. Thus, at the 17th Games there were 20 team-members from Kiev, at 19th—27, and at the 21st—54.

Kiev is proud to be playing host to competitors and guests to the 1980 Olympics. An enormous programme of preparatory work has been carried out for this honourable occasion. Practically all the city's stadiums have been modernised and a large number of new sports facilities have been constructed.

A major undertaking has been the reconstruction of the Central Stadium, where the Olympic football preliminary rounds will be played. This stadium was built shortly before the last war and has been reconstructed on a number of occasions since. This giant sports centre has been thoroughly reconstructed for the 1980 Olympics in accordance with modern requirements. The football field has been completely relaid. A new draining system and underground heating make it possible to maintain the field in excellent repair regardless of the whims of the

A sports parade on Kreshchatik

The Spartak women's handball team, many-times USSR champion and holder of the European Champions' Cup

When a favourite team plays

The Dynamo Stadium pool

The Kiev Sokol ice-hockey team in action

Along the vast expanses of the Dnieper

weather. The lighting in the stadium has been greatly improved. The old 35-metre floodlight masts have been replaced by masts 82 metres high. These are fitted with powerful floodlights, whose candlepower meets the IOC requirements and makes possible high quality colour TV coverage. The lower level of the stands has been changed and placed on a concrete foundation. The central pavilion has also been thoroughly reconstructed, and now houses changing rooms, judges' rooms and service premises. The pavilion has acquired two more storeys, and all

Oleg Blokhin, the Kiev Dynamo soccer team's famous forward

Participants in a track-and-field meet between the USA, USSR and Bulgaria in Kiev

the changing rooms have small swimming pools. Rooms have been equipped for officials, such as representatives from the IOC and the FIFA. The pavilion contains medical rooms and massage rooms.

A considerable area of the new pavilion at the Central Stadium is taken up by a press centre. The journalists who will come here to cover the Olympic preliminaries will not experience the least inconveniences. Here, in the information centre, they will be able to receive the most varied information about the competitors, and about events at the other Olympic centres. Photographers will be

Merited Master of Sport of the USSR Irina Deryugina, world champion in rhythmic gymnastics, after a successful performance

The Stroitel basketball team during a USSR championship match

Merited Master of Sport of the USSR, Olympic champion Yuri Sedykh

A relay-race

able to have their films developed in the laboratories housed in pavilion. Comfortable commentators' cabins have been fitted for radio and TV correspondents. A modern communications centre is attached to the press centre. The journalists will have at their disposal bars and cafés.

The Dynamo stadium has also been considerably modernised, along with the Spartak, Lokomotiv, and Army Sports Club stadiums, which will provide excellent training facilities for the Olympic contestants.

A sports centre has been set up for the Olympians in the Kiev suburb of Koncha-Zaspa, in a pine forest on the banks of the Dnieper. Here the competitors will find all they need for the purposes of leisure and training: comfortable hotel rooms with all conveniences, saunas, a medical centre, gymnasiums, a pool, and open-air sports grounds. The sports centre is linked to the city by a speedway, the journey to the stadium taking no more than 20 minutes.

The city's guests will find it interesting to visit Kiev's other sports facilities, such as the Kiev Palace of Sport. In a matter of minutes its hall can be converted into an ice rink, into basketball courts or into a concert stage.

The Kiev fencing school has produced many famous masters

Kiev can boast of many more remarkable sports areas. Along the broad blue expanses of the Dnieper the visitor will see fragile canoes, powerful hydrofoils and graceful, white-sailed yachts. The triumphs of Kiev oarsmen and yachtsmen are widely known. This is one of the reasons for the growing popularity of the smooth waters of the Matveyevsky creek and the Rusanovka canal as a venue for major regattas.

The inhabitants of Kiev have done their best to ensure a hospitable welcome for the Olympians, coaches, journalists and tourists, to supply all their needs throughout the Olympic events, and give them every possible opportunity for sightseeing and leisure. New luxury hotels are rising in the Ukrainian capital for this purpose, to be ready to receive their first guests by the opening of the 1980 Olympics.

Special medical establishments are set aside for Olympians and visitors. Several new service stations and carparks are to be made

A rowing contest in Matveyevsky Cove

The Kiev racecourse

available to tourists who come by car. An extensive cultural programme has also been planned. All the best theatres in Kiev as well as the Ukraine's leading orchestras, song and dance companies will give performances during the period of the Olympic Games.

The development of sport in Kiev is such that we can be sure of seeing a large number of its residents participating in the 1980 contests. The Soviet Olympic team will include track and field athletes, swimmers, footballers, wrestlers, basketball and handball players, scullers, canoeists, fencers and exponents of many other sports. There are 218 Kiev athletes in the country's Olympic reserve.

KIEV IN 24 HOURS

We invite those of our foreign guests whose stay in Kiev is brief to choose amongst the following Intourist coach tours:

1. Kiev—capital of the Ukrainian SSR
2. The city's architectural and historical monuments
3. Sporting Kiev
4. Kiev's construction sites

TOUR NO. 1

This tour will acquaint our guests with the history of Kiev from its very origins, showing them round the celebrated landmarks of the Ukrainian capital's revolutionary past, of its war experiences and peace-time achievements, they will see for themselves how its present-day inhabitants live, what their aspirations and plans for the future are. The tour starts on Vladimir Hill, which overlooks the city's left bank and the Dnieper plain. From here it proceeds through the territory of ancient Kiev, along its central thoroughfares, where the theatres, concert halls, museums, institutes, cultural centres, sports facilities, major hotels and shopping centres are to be found. The visitors will also see the buildings which house the republic's supreme organs of power and the Hero City's numerous monuments. From here they will cross the Dnieper into the new housing estates and visit the sweeping leisure zone on the islands in the Dnieper.

The route of the tour is as follows: Vladimir Hill—Bogdan Khmelnitsky Square—St. Sophia Cathedral—the Golden Gates—Taras Shevchenko Opera and Ballet Theatre—Presidium of the Ukrainian Academy of Sciences—Taras Shevchenko University—Central Stadium—Red Army St.—Kreshchatik St.—Monument to Lenin—Leninist Komsomol Square—the Philharmonic building—CPSU Library—Dnipro Hotel—Monument to G. Petrovsky—Kirov St.—Council of Ministers of the Ukrainian SSR—Supreme Soviet of the Ukrainian SSR—Soviet Square—Monument to N. Vatutin—Monument to the Heroes of October—Monument to the Arsenal Revolutionary Workers—January Uprising St.—Park of Eternal Glory—Monument to the Unknown Soldier—N. Ostrovsky Young Pioneer and Schoolchildren's Palace—Park of Askold's Grave—Metro Bridge—Hydropark—Rusanovka housing estate—Slavutich Hotel—Y. Paton Bridge—V. Primakov Park—Park Road—Kreshchatik St.

TOUR NO. 2

This tour includes visits to two of the most famous architectural complexes of the city, ranging from the 11th to the 18th century—the St. Sophia State Architectural Historical Museum and the Kiev-Pechery Lavra.

The tour takes the following route: Bogdan Khmelnitsky Square—St. Sophia Museum—Kalinin Square—October Revolution Square—Kreshchatik St.—Kirov St.—January Uprising St.—Kiev-Pechery Lavra (Trinity Gate Church—Lavra Great Belfry—Cathedral of the Dormition—Church of the Saviour in Berestovo—Kovnir Building—Museum of Historical Treasures—Refectory—Museum of Ukrainian Folk Art—Near or Far Caves)—Kreshchatik St.

TOUR NO. 3

This tour will take our foreign guests around the city's major sports facilities, including the Central Stadium, venue for the preliminary rounds of the 1980 Olympic football tournament. The guests will be told about the development of sport in the Ukraine, about the achievements of Ukrainian athletes, about the facilities available for Soviet citizens' sporting and leisure pastimes and about the training of athletes.

The tour will take the following route: Central Stadium—Rus Hotel—Palace of Sports—Red Army St.—Monument to Lenin—Institute of Physical Education—Ukraina Palace of Culture—40 Years of October Avenue—New Complex of Shevchenko University—Racecourse—Ice Stadium—Exhibition of Economic Achievements of the Ukrainian SSR—Goloseyevsky Park—Science Avenue—Friendship of Peoples' Boulevard—Y. Paton Bridge—Bereznyaki housing estate—Indoor Athletics Arena—Rusanovka housing estate—Hydropark—Metro Bridge—Dnieper Embankment—Vladimirsky Spusk (Hill)—Dynamo Stadium.

TOUR NO. 4

On the Observation Platform of the Young Pioneer Park, which gives a panoramic view of the new town, the visitors will be given an interesting account of the history of Kiev's growth, and about the Master Plan for the city's future development, which reaches right up to the year 2000. This tour will take in new housing estates on both sides of the Dnieper, familiarising the visitor with modern building and town planning methods, with the special features of the city's landscape and its natural environment. During the tour they will see the new TV centre with its 387-metre tower and will visit Babi Yar, the site of a memorial to the victims of the nazi invasion.

The tour takes the following route:

Leninist Komsomol Square—Young Pioneer Park Observation Platform—Vladimirsky Spusk—Pochtovaya Square—Dnieper Embankment—Y. Paton Bridge—Rusanovka Embankment—Levoberezhnaya (Letf Bank) Metro station—Komsomolskaya Metro station—Moscow Bridge—M. Zalka St.—Vinogradar housing estate—Babi Yar Memorial Complex.

INTOURIST WELCOMES YOU TO KIEV

The Kiev branch of Intourist, USSR Company for Foreign Travel, invites foreign visitors to Kiev to stay in the modern luxury hotels Dnipro, Lybid, Rus and those who come by car in the Prolisok motel and camping site.

Intourist organises:

—individual and group tours of the city, to museums and exhibitions;

—hikes along the Dnieper;

—visits to concerts and theatres;

—excursions to the town of Cherkassy;

—excursions by boat and bus to the town of Kanev visiting the grave of the great Ukrainian poet Taras Shevchenko;

—excursions to the town of Chernigov visiting architectural landmarks of the 11th to 18th centuries and the house-museum of the Ukrainian writer M. Kotsyubinsky;

—trips out of town, picnics in the country;

—visits to restaurants specialising in Ukrainian cuisine and wines: Khata Karasya, Vitryak, Natalka, Verkhovina, Dubki, Kureni, Mlyn;

—visits to the Finnish baths, bowling alley.

Intourist offers for hire chauffeur-driven Volga cars, as well as self-drive Volgas and Zhigulis.

Intourist sells:

—tours to the cities of the Soviet Union;

—plane, train and boat tickets;

—petrol and oil coupons.

Intourist will organise international phone calls.

For the information of our guests: the hotels Dnipro (Ploshchad Leninskovo Komsomola), Lybid (Ploshchad Pobedy) and Rus (21, Ulitsa Kuibysheva) all have bars open daily from 8 p.m. to 2 a.m.

Dear visitors to Kiev, we ask you to phone the following numbers to find about additional services provided by these hotels:

Dnipro—290989

Lybid—742066

Intourist —245976; 255397

Prolisok—440093

We hope you thoroughly enjoy your stay in our city and come away with the best impressions.

INTOURBUREAU OFFERS ITS SERVICES

Every year Kiev is visited by large numbers of foreign tourists who come through the USSR Central Council of Trade Unions in accordance with programmes based on agreements with the trade union organisations of socialist countries as well as travel firms and public organisations of capitalist countries working under the auspices of trade unions. These guests are attended to by the Intourbureau of the Kiev City Council for Tourism and Excursions.

Intourbureau accommodates its guests in comfortable hotels, for the most part situated on the picturesque left bank of the Dnieper and linked to the centre by the Metro and other forms of transport.

The guests have at their service the Yunost, Gorishche and Kazbek restaurants; here they will be able to order their own national dishes as well as those of Ukrainian cuisine.

The production complex of the Kiev City Council for Tourism and Excursions offers its guests a range of souvenirs—badges, pennants, sew-on badges and many others, decorated with sporting and Ukrainian symbols.

We ask you to address all enquiries to the address:

5 Friendship of Peoples Boulevard (Bulvar Druzhby Narodov), Druzhba Hotel, tel. 687550.

SPUTNIK AT YOUR SERVICE

The emblem of the Soviet young people's travel organisation—a sputnik soaring above the earth—is well-known all over the world.

The Ukrainian branches of Sputnik are working hard to develop tourism amongst young people, and at present have more than 40 regional and city bureaux of international young people's tourism, as well as its international youth centres—Sputnik in Gurzuf, Verkhovina in Uzhgorod, and Mir in Kiev.

Every new year brings an increase in the volume and scope of international young people's tourism. At the present time Sputnik is cooperating with 400 youth, student, trade union and tourist organisations of 70 countries. The majority of its tourist exchanges are with the socialist countries. Tourist organisations of capitalist countries are also to be found amongst Sputnik's traditional partners.

Sputnik's Mir youth tourist centre in Kiev is situated next to the Goloseyevsky Park named after M. Rylsky. When its high-rise hotel block is put into operation it will be able to accommodate 800 tourists at a time. The guests will have at their convenience single, double and triple rooms, luxury suites, two restaurants, cafés, a bar and a modern sauna complete with pool. An interesting and varied programme will be laid on for their stay in the Mir centre, including evenings of international friendship, meetings with leading Soviet athletes, round-table discussions and debates, lectures in foreign languages, improvised concerts and film festivals.

Sputnik arranges:

— *accommodation in tourist class hotels;*

— *coach, rail and car transport;*

— *a 50 per cent reduction on rail travel;*

— *a 30 per cent reduction on air travel for the period between October 1 and April 25;*

— *reductions on tickets to museums, art galleries and lecture halls;*

— *qualified interpreter-guides.*

The programme for foreign tourists' stay in our country which has been carefully prepared and worked out by the Sputnik travel bureau acquaints our guests with the life of the Soviet people in all its breadth and variety.

Sputnik is always glad to welcome old and new friends!

Address all enquiries to the address: Kiev 25, 4 Ulitsa Chkalova, tel. 245084; telex 132164.

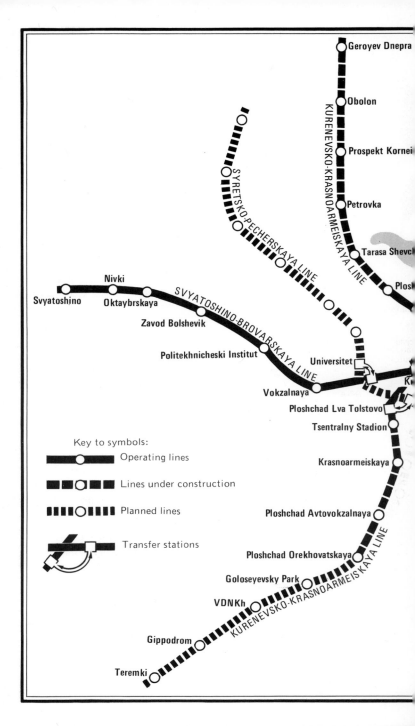

Geroyev Dnepra

Obolon

Prospekt Kornei

Petrovka

KURENEVSKO-KRASNOARMEISKAYA LINE

Tarasa Shevcl

Plosh

SYRETSKO-PECHERSKAYA LINE

Nivki

Svyatoshino

Oktaybrskaya

SVYATOSHINO-BROVARSKAYA LINE

Zavod Bolshevik

Politekhnicheski Institut

Universitet

K

Vokzalnaya

Ploshchad Lva Tolstovo

Tsentralny Stadion

Krasnoarmeiskaya

Key to symbols:

Operating lines

Lines under construction

Planned lines

Transfer stations

Ploshchad Avtovokzalnaya

Ploshchad Orekhovatskaya

KURENEVSKO-KRASNOARMEISKAYA LINE

Goloseyevsky Park

VDNKh

Gippodrom

Teremki

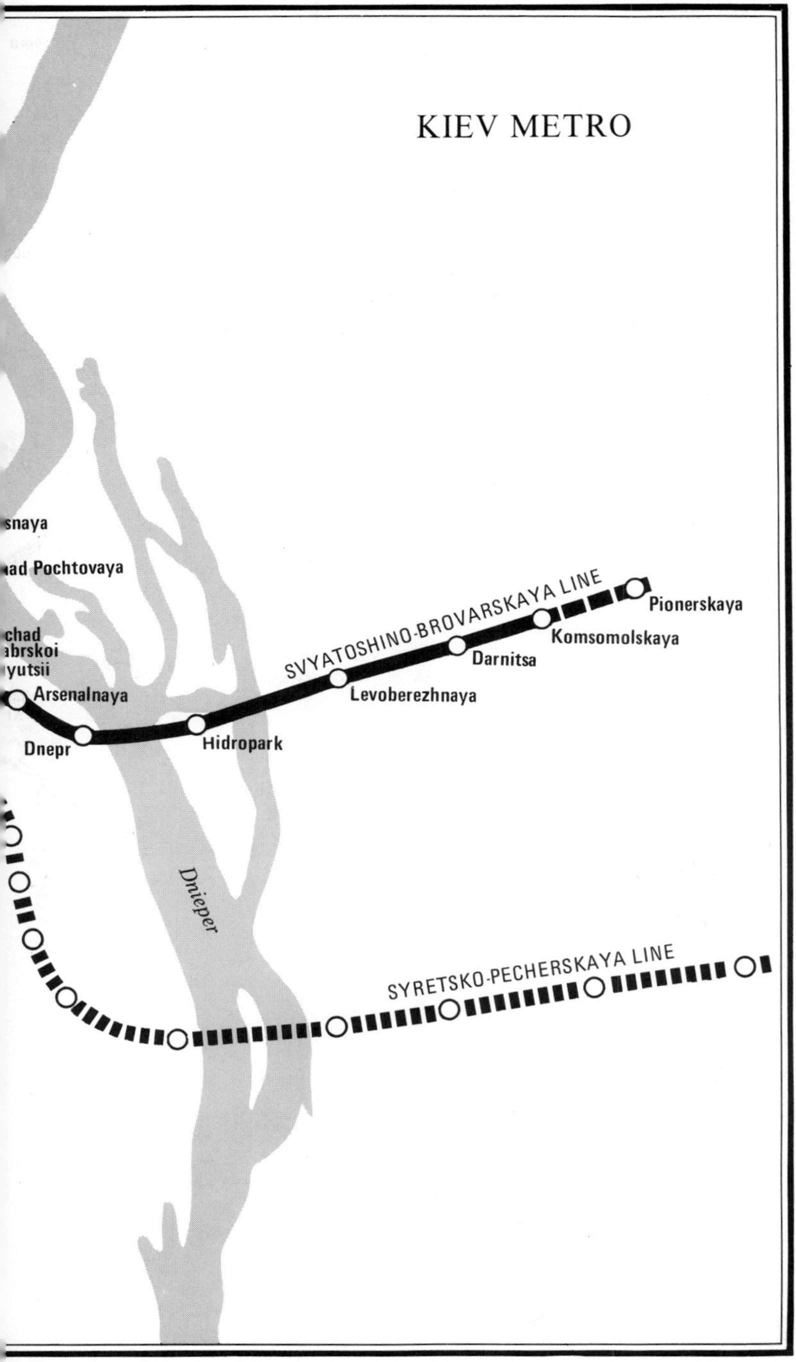

KIEV METRO

snaya

ad Pochtovaya

chad
abrskoi
yutsii

Arsenalnaya

Dnepr

SVYATOSHINO-BROVARSKAYA LINE

Hidropark

Levoberezhnaya

Darnitsa

Komsomolskaya

Pionerskaya

Dnieper

SYRETSKO-PECHERSKAYA LINE

SOUVENIRS TO BUY

Guests to Kiev will find a wide range of souvenirs in the city's shops to satisfy everyone's taste.

Amongst the goods available for purchase are gold jewellery, silver and cupro-nickel cutlery, crystal ware, exquisite necklaces, pendants, earrings, rings with precious stones such as diamonds, sapphires and emeralds.

Ukrainian embroidery enjoys great popularity. Whatever the current fashion, embroidery never goes out of style. Embroidered tablecloths, napkins, Ukrainian towels, curtains, shirts, blouses, skirts, bedspreads and carpets are brightly decorated with Ukrainian motifs.

Our guests' attention is always drawn by Ukrainian ceramic wares. Pots, bowls, and clay figurines never fail to delight connoisseurs of this original form of applied art.

Ukrainian wood carvings provide another sort of unusual souvenir, illustrating another area of folk art. The visitor will find a great variety of boxes, plates, and statuettes decorated with detailed ornament.

The famous Kosov inlaid souvenirs represent a marvellous combination of different types of wood and metal, horn, mother-of-pearl and beadwork.

The shops also offer Soviet-made radio and photographic wares which are outstanding for their high quality and reliability; fur garments from silver fox, astrakhan, polar fox, mink, musquash and sable; confectionary and liqueurs, and caviar.

Guests will find all these goods and souvenirs in the Kashtan department store on 24/26 Bulvar Lesi Ukrainki, tel. 956127, in kiosks in the hotels Dnipro, Lybid, Rus and the Prolisok motel, at Borispol Airport, in the St. Sophia museum and the Kiev-Pechery Lavra as well as in art shops. These are situated at the following addresses: 12 Ulitsa Lenina; 27 Ulitsa Lenina; 41 Krasnoarmeyskaya Ulitsa; 17 Ulitsa Entuziastov.

A visit to one of these salons will be sure to leave the foreign guest to our city impressed by the artistry and talent of the Ukrainian people, and the souvenirs he acquires will serve as a permanent reminder of his pleasant stay in the capital of the Soviet Ukraine.

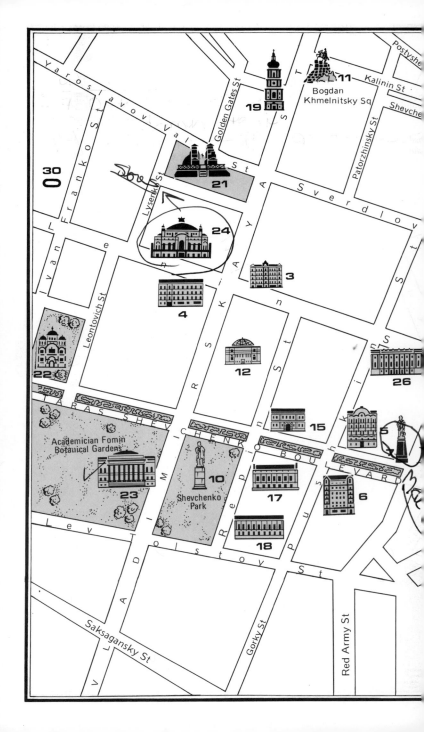

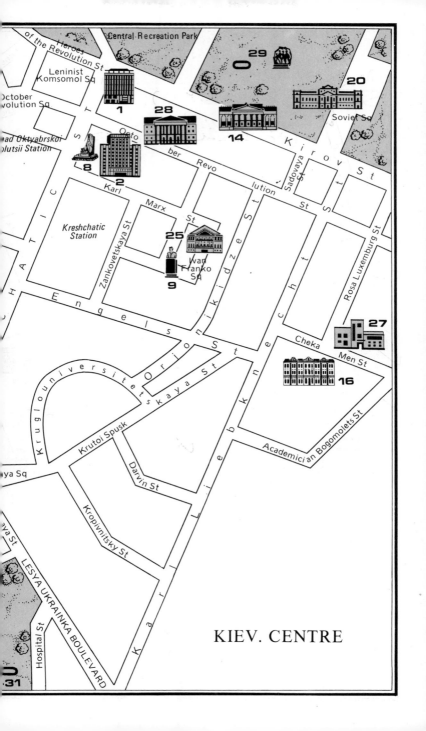

KIEV. CENTRE

KIEV
(City Centre)

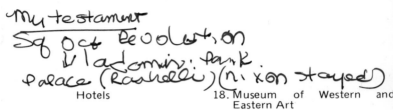

My testament
Sq Oct Revolution
Vladomir. tank.
Palace (Rastrelli) (nixon stayed)

Hotels

1. Dnepr
2. Moskva
3. Intourist
4. Teatralnaya
5. Leningradskaya
6. Ukraina

Monuments

7. Monument to V. I. Lenin
8. Monument in honour of the Great October Socialist Revolution
9. Monument to Ivan Franko
10. Monument to Taras Shevchenko
11. Monument to Bogdan Khmelnitsky

Museum

12. Kiev branch of the Central Lenin Museum
13. Taras Shevchenko House-Museum
14. Museum of Ukrainian Fine Arts of the Ukrainian SSR
15. Shevchenko Museum
16. Museum of the History of the Great Patriotic War of 1941-1945
17. Museum of Russian Art

18. Museum of Western and Eastern Art

Historical and Architectural Monuments

19. St. Sophia Cathedral Museum
20. Mariinsky Palace
21. Golden Gates
22. St. Vladimir Cathedral
23. Shevchenko University

Teatres and Concert Halls

24. Shevchenko Opera and Ballet Theatre
25. Ivan Franko Ukrainian Drama Theatre
26. Lesya Ukrainka Russian Drama Theatre
27. Leninist Komsomol Theatre for Young Spectators
28. Oktyabrsky Palace of Culture

Sports Facilities

29. Dynamo Stadium and monument to the Dynamo soccer players who were shot by the nazis
30. Cycling Track
31. Central Stadium
32. Sports Palace

Request to Readers

Progress Publishers would be glad to have your opinion of this book, its translation and design and any suggestions you may have for future publications.

Please send all your comments to 17, Zubovsky Boulevard, Moscow, USSR.

ИБ № 7588

Редактор русского текста *В. В. Остроумов*
Контрольный редактор *Г. А. Павлов*
Художник *Н. В. Нестеренко*
Художественный редактор *Я. А. Маликов*
Технический редактор *Г. Н. Калинцева*

Сдано в набор 18.4.1979г. Подписано в печать 11.7. 1979г.
Формат 84 × 108 1/32 Бумага офсетная мелованная Гарнитура «Столетие»
Печать офсетная Условн.печ.л. 10,08 Уч.–изд.л. 11,32
Тираж 110 000 экз. Заказ № 005 Цена 1 руб. 90 коп. Изд. № 28798

Издательство «Прогресс» Государственного комитета СССР по делам издательств,
полиграфии и книжной торговли.
Москва, 119021, Зубовский бульвар, 17

«Ланд ог Фольк» Дания

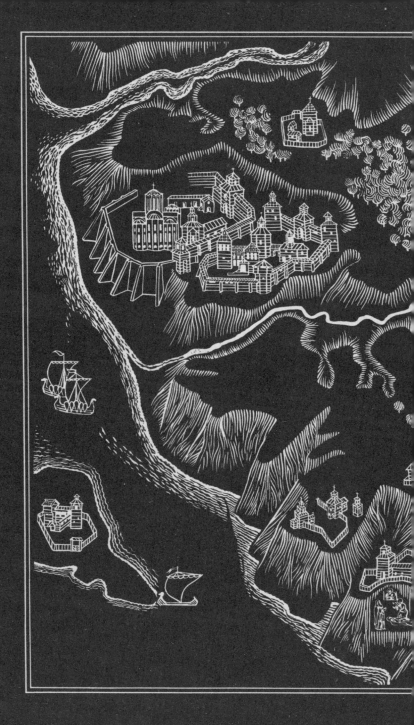